Spanish Word Games

FOR

DUMMIES®

D1648851

by Adam Cohen and Leslie Frates

WILEY

Wiley Publishing, Inc.

Spanish Word Games For Dummies®

Published by
Wiley Publishing, Inc.
111 River St.
Hoboken, NJ 07030-5774
www.wiley.com

Copyright © 2010 by Wiley Publishing, Inc., Indianapolis, Indiana

Published by Wiley Publishing, Inc., Indianapolis, Indiana

Published simultaneously in Canada

No part of this publication may be reproduced, stored in a retrieval system or transmitted in any form or by any means, electronic, mechanical, photocopying, recording, scanning or otherwise, except as permitted under Sections 107 or 108 of the 1976 United States Copyright Act, without either the prior written permission of the Publisher, or authorization through payment of the appropriate per-copy fee to the Copyright Clearance Center, 222 Rosewood Drive, Danvers, MA 01923, (978) 750-8400, fax (978) 646-8600. Requests to the Publisher for permission should be addressed to the Permissions Department, John Wiley & Sons, Inc., 111 River Street, Hoboken, NJ 07030, (201) 748-6011, fax (201) 748-6008, or online at http://www.wiley.com/go/permissions.

Trademarks: Wiley, the Wiley Publishing logo, For Dummies, the Dummies Man logo, A Reference for the Rest of Us!, The Dummies Way, Dummies Daily, The Fun and Easy Way, Dummies.com, Making Everything Easier, and related trade dress are trademarks or registered trademarks of John Wiley & Sons, Inc. and/or its affiliates in the United States and other countries, and may not be used without written permission. All other trademarks are the property of their respective owners. Wiley Publishing, Inc., is not associated with any product or vendor mentioned in this book.

LIMIT OF LIABILITY/DISCLAIMER OF WARRANTY: THE PUBLISHER AND THE AUTHOR MAKE NO REPRESENTATIONS OR WARRANTIES WITH RESPECT TO THE ACCURACY OR COMPLETENESS OF THE CONTENTS OF THIS WORK AND SPECIFICALLY DISCLAIM ALL WARRANTIES, INCLUDING WITHOUT LIMITATION WARRANTIES OF FITNESS FOR A PARTICULAR PURPOSE. NO WARRANTY MAY BE CREATED OR EXTENDED BY SALES OR PROMOTIONAL MATERIALS. THE ADVICE AND STRATEGIES CONTAINED HEREIN MAY NOT BE SUITABLE FOR EVERY SITUATION. THIS WORK IS SOLD WITH THE UNDERSTANDING THAT THE PUBLISHER IS NOT ENGAGED IN RENDERING LEGAL, ACCOUNTING, OR OTHER PROFESSIONAL SERVICES. IF PROFESSIONAL ASSISTANCE IS REQUIRED, THE SERVICES OF A COMPETENT PROFESSIONAL PERSON SHOULD BE SOUGHT. NEITHER THE PUBLISHER NOR THE AUTHOR SHALL BE LIABLE FOR DAMAGES ARISING HEREFROM. THE FACT THAT AN ORGANIZATION OR WEBSITE IS REFERRED TO IN THIS WORK AS A CITATION AND/OR A POTENTIAL SOURCE OF FURTHER INFORMATION DOES NOT MEAN THAT THE AUTHOR OR THE PUBLISHER ENDORSES THE INFORMATION THE ORGANIZATION OR WEBSITE MAY PROVIDE OR RECOMMENDATIONS IT MAY MAKE. FURTHER, READERS SHOULD BE AWARE THAT INTERNET WEBSITES LISTED IN THIS WORK MAY HAVE CHANGED OR DISAPPEARED BETWEEN WHEN THIS WORK WAS WRITTEN AND WHEN IT IS READ.

For general information on our other products and services, please contact our Customer Care Department within the U.S. at 877-762-2974, outside the U.S. at 317-572-3993, or fax 317-572-4002.

For technical support, please visit www.wiley.com/techsupport.

Wiley also publishes its books in a variety of electronic formats. Some content that appears in print may not be available in electronic books.

Library of Congress Control Number: 2009939790

ISBN: 978-0-470-50200-6

Manufactured in the United States of America

10 9 8 7 6 5 4 3 2 1

WILEY

R0439935066

About the Authors

Adam Cohen first encountered puzzles in the *New York Post,* where as a young child he regularly savored the Uncle Art's Funland puzzle feature. He later discovered the *Post*'s Wonderword and the crossword puzzle, and was so hooked he tried construct- ing them on his own. He was 15 when his first crossword was published in his high school newspaper, where he served as a regular contributor for two years. He has since graduated to news- papers such as *The New York Times, Newsday,* and the *New York Sun* (where he also served as a test-solver); *Games* and *World of Puzzles* magazines; and the *Uncle John's Bathroom Reader* series of puzzle books. In 2007, in his capacity as an employee of John Wiley & Sons, he constructed the crossword puzzle for the company's bicentennial *festschrift* volume *Knowledge for Generations*. In addi- tion to constructing puzzles, Adam is a proofreader and editor for publishers of puzzle books. He is currently the associate editor of *Puzzler Brain Trainer* magazine, and a proofreader for the *Mind Stretchers* book series, published by Reader's Digest.

Listening to his mother (for once), Adam decided to study Spanish instead of German in high school and quickly fell in love with the language and culture. He placed in the National Spanish Examinations from 1987–1989 and 1991, and he was a contributor and editor to his high school's foreign language magazine *Polyglot*. For a Spanish sophomore-year public speaking assignment, he gave a talk on how to construct crossword puzzles, which synthe- sized two of his major interests and foreshadowed this book by about 20 years. He continued his studies by minoring in Spanish at the University of Pennsylvania.

When he isn't constructing or editing puzzles, Adam enjoys games — particularly those involving words, trivia, or casino chips — reading, movies, swimming, photography, and travel.

Adam was born, raised, and currently lives in Brooklyn, New York.

Leslie Frates didn't grow up in a Spanish-speaking home but fell in love with the language when she was in first grade and decided in second grade that she wanted to be a Spanish teacher. Leslie has been living her dream, teaching Spanish for over 30 years, and currently is a lecturer at California State University, East Bay. She received her bachelor's degree in Spanish from CSUEB (back when it was known as Cal State Hayward), and her master's degree in Spanish from UC Berkeley.

Leslie has been a game and puzzle aficionada since childhood and met coauthor Adam Cohen at the American Crossword Puzzle Tournament in 2007. She parlayed her lifelong nerdiness into becoming a five-time undefeated champion on the TV game show *Jeopardy!* in 1991.

When not teaching or puzzling, Leslie enjoys doing counted cross-stitch, watching old movies on Netflix, and visiting her favorite city, Chicago.

Leslie is married to Bob, an attorney. Her son, Leland, is in graduate school, and has no interest in either Spanish or puzzles.

Dedication

From Adam:

To Hunter College High School in New York City, especially

- José Díaz, my first Spanish teacher, who introduced me to this beautiful language and culture with scholarship, dedication, and wit.
- The editorial staff of *What's What,* the newspaper that published my first crossword, for providing me with the first of many creative outlets for puzzles.

From Leslie:

To my parents, who supported and encouraged me in my nerdiness, dreams, and goals; bought that wondrous volume-a-week encyclopedia at the grocery store, which gave me my first keys to knowledge and a lifelong love of learning; and always let me sit under the cork tree and be happy.

To my husband, Bob, my best friend and biggest cheerleader, who is always by my side, giving me everything I ever hoped for.

To my son, Leland, who is our dream come true.

Authors' Acknowledgments

From Adam:

Sincerest gratitude must first go to Patrick Berry, for recommending me for this project.

This book would never have been realized without the guidance and support of Wiley's professional staff: Acquisitions Editor Lindsay Lefevere, Project Editor Traci Cumbay, and Technical Reviewers Denise Sutherland and Alicia Añino.

In addition, I must acknowledge the assistance of Todd McClary, for his cogent and thoughtful feedback on Chapter 2; Shawn Kennedy, whose software saved me hours of grunt work on the cryptogram puzzles; and Trip Payne, for helpful discussions on puzzle construction.

Last, and certainly not least, I must thank my dear friend and coauthor Leslie Frates. Little did I know when I watched her on *Jeopardy!* nearly 20 years ago that not only would we meet in person, but that we would have the privilege of writing this book together. Her counsel and contributions were invaluable; she looked over everything I did and made it better. I can't thank her enough.

From Leslie:

I thank Señor Jackson, my Spanish teacher in the second grade, who ignited in a little non-Hispanic girl in Hayward, California, the spark of Hispanophilia that has never dimmed, and who made me want to be a Spanish teacher, too.

I thank all my teachers along the way who inspired, enlightened, and informed me and have given me the opportunity to experience the joy of teaching, learning, and knowing.

The guidance and support of Acquisitions Editor Lindsay Lefevere, Project Editor Traci Cumbay, and Technical Reviewers Denise Sutherland and Alicia Añino gave me the confidence to bring this book to fruition.

The best thing about this entire project was, is, and will always be my loving friendship with Adam Cohen, whose faith in me, understanding, and enthusiasm can never be repaid in equal measure. There are not enough words of thanks in any language to express my gratitude to him.

Publisher's Acknowledgments

We're proud of this book; please send us your comments at http://dummies.custhelp.com. For other comments, please contact our Customer Care Department within the U.S. at 877-762-2974, outside the U.S. at 317-572-3993, or fax 317-572-4002.

Some of the people who helped bring this book to market include the following:

Acquisitions, Editorial, and Media Development

Project Editor: Traci Cumbay

Acquisitions Editor: Lindsay Lefevere

Copy Editor: Traci Cumbay

Assistant Editor: Erin Calligan Mooney

Editorial Program Coordinator: Joe Niesen

Technical Editors: Alicia Añino, Denise Sutherland

Senior Editorial Manager: Jennifer Ehrlich

Editorial Supervisor and Reprint Editor: Carmen Krikorian

Editorial Assistants: David Lutton, Jennette ElNaggar

Cartoons: Rich Tennant (www.the5thwave.com)

Composition Services

Project Coordinator: Patrick Redmond

Layout and Graphics: Brooke Graczyk, Julie Trippetti, Erin Zeltner

Proofreaders: ConText Editorial Services, Inc., Jessica Kramer

---

Publishing and Editorial for Consumer Dummies

Diane Graves Steele, Vice President and Publisher, Consumer Dummies

Kristin Ferguson-Wagstaffe, Product Development Director, Consumer Dummies

Ensley Eikenburg, Associate Publisher, Travel

Kelly Regan, Editorial Director, Travel

Publishing for Technology Dummies

Andy Cummings, Vice President and Publisher, Dummies Technology/General User

Composition Services

Debbie Stailey, Director of Composition Services

Contents at a Glance

Table of Contents

Introduction

*W*hile you were growing up, you acquired your native language (or languages) without any formal training or instruction. Your parents may have taught you the names of certain objects — animals, colors, or shapes, maybe — but they probably never sat down with you when you were a toddler and went over verb conjugation tables with you, or explained to you when to use *a* and when to use *an,* or why you pronounce the English word spelled *knight* as if it were *nite.*

In fact, without even realizing it, you spent much of your early years acquiring your native language by exploring your environment, by listening to and repeating the sounds around you, and even by babbling. While you were engaging in activities that may have seemed like play, you were actually focusing your energies on language acquisition.

If you study a second language, you probably do so in a much different fashion: maybe sitting in a classroom, writing exercises in a workbook, or memorizing lessons from a textbook. As much as you might enjoy these endeavors, we venture a guess that more traditionally fun activities, such as word games and puzzles, are a small part of your language-learning curriculum, if they're included at all.

In addition to being fun, puzzles and word games stimulate your brain (and evidence increasingly suggests that such stimulation may forestall the onset of conditions such as Alzheimer's disease). Engaging repeatedly in mentally stimulating activities is no doubt cerebrally nutritious, but activities that are different and approach things from new perspectives are particularly beneficial, because the brain loves novelty. Learning a new language, or taking a refresher course on what you might have learned a while ago, certainly qualifies as a novel activity. And learning a language using puzzles as a vehicle hits the trifecta: stimulation, novelty, and fun.

About This Book

If you're a student of Spanish, you might wish that there were more lively and creative alternatives to some of the traditional vehicles of language learning, such as rote memorization, workbook exercises, or practice dialogs. We don't begrudge these techniques; indeed, the best way to learn a language (or just about anything else for that matter) is to present the material in a variety of different formats.

This book offers that lively and creative alternative, serving as another tool in your language-learning toolbox. It presents Spanish puzzles and word games specifically designed to reinforce Spanish sounds, spelling patterns, and vocabulary words as a means to help you improve your Spanish speaking, writing, and reading skills. While the puzzles are largely grouped according to subject matter, we did not structure this book as a traditional textbook, nor is it intended to serve as one. Jump in wherever you like. Do whatever puzzle grabs you at the moment. Enjoy yourself. (And if that means working straight through from front cover to back, then please be our guest.)

Foolish Assumptions

In order to write this book, we had to make a few assumptions about who you might be. We assume that you

- ✔ Have a basic familiarity with Spanish vocabulary and grammar.

- ✔ Would like to reinforce or improve your language skills.

- ✔ Have a curiosity about or interest in puzzles or word games; familiarity with them is helpful but not essential.

- ✔ Want to have fun!

Whether you're a current student of Spanish looking for some stimulating ways to spice up your classroom lessons, haven't studied Spanish in years but want to brush up your language skills in novel ways for your upcoming trip to Spain, or are a native speaker just looking for some fun linguistic challenges, the puzzles in this book reinforce your Spanish skills and strengthen your brain in a stimulating and entertaining way.

How This Book Is Organized

So that you can easily navigate this book, the upcoming sections describe briefly what you find within it.

Part 1: Building Your Spanish Skills with Word Games

The two chapters in this section provide a foundation for approaching the puzzles in this book for fun and education. Chapter 1 shows you why puzzles are effective vehicles for improving your Spanish, and Chapter 2 helps you hone your solving skills so that you get the most out of the puzzles and learn as much Spanish as you can.

Part II: The Puzzles

If Part I is the appetizer, then Part II is the main course. Here you find more than 100 Spanish word games and puzzles. We divided them into chapters based on subject matter, and each puzzle focuses on a different topic. These puzzles engage you in a variety of formats that ask you not just to translate words from English to Spanish or vice versa but to think in Spanish, as well.

Part III: The Solutions

This section contains the answers to the puzzles in Part II. Check your work, brush up on translations, or take a peek at the answer that has you stumped.

Part IV: The Part of Tens

The puzzle challenges in Chapter 11 give your brain a strenuous workout. They include novel puzzle types and combinations of puzzle types featured elsewhere in this book. Because the words within the puzzles aren't organized by topic, the puzzles reflect the kind of real-world challenges a new speaker faces. The answers to the puzzles appear at the end of the chapter.

Chapter 12 contains additional practical tools and creative suggestions to help you continue to improve your Spanish capabilities.

Icons Used in This Book

The icons in the margins direct you to information that we feel is particularly worth noting. Here's what you find next to each of the icons we use:

Important details that you're likely to return to again and again as you work through the puzzles or continue your Spanish studies appear next to this icon.

You find this icon next to information that can save you time or enhance your puzzle and Spanish-language pursuits.

Where to Go from Here

You can approach this book in a number of different ways. If you're interested in how puzzles can improve your Spanish, Chapter 1 is a good place to start. If you'd like more information about the different puzzle types in this book, with tips and strategies to help you approach them, we suggest beginning with Chapter 2. (And dive back into Chapter 2 whenever you get stuck or need to review basic solving techniques.)

If you're ready to tackle the puzzles head on, flip straight to Part II. The puzzles are organized by subject matter, and so you can concentrate on those topics that interest you. For example, if you'd like to review some introductory Spanish concepts, you may want to look at Chapter 3 first. If you're particularly interested in puzzles about Spanish culture, Chapter 8 might be a good starting point. If, on the other hand, you want to tackle the puzzles sequentially, we wouldn't dream of dissuading you.

This is your book and your experience; approach it however you see fit. Feel free to use this book in whatever way you find educational and fun!

Part I
Building Your Spanish Skills with Word Games

The 5th Wave   By Rich Tennant

"He hasn't solved any of the Spanish word games, but that doesn't mean he isn't building his vocabulary."

In this part...

*U*sing puzzles to master Spanish or refresh your skills
comes with a lot of benefits. In Chapter 1, we tell you
about them. Chapter 2 describes all the puzzle types you
encounter in the book, and gives you tips and strategies for
solving each one.

Chapter 1

Mastering Spanish through Word Games and Puzzles

In This Chapter

▶ Finding — and harnessing — your motivation

▶ Building new brain capacity

▶ Making the most of your studies

*Y*ou have some Spanish floating around in your head, and it's not just the kind that you see on the menu of your favorite *taquería* or fast-food restaurant. Maybe you're taking a class right now, or maybe you took some Spanish in high school or college a million years ago. Maybe Spanish is linked to a hazy memory of childhood, of speaking with a relative or family friend from the mother country; perhaps you have Spanish-speaking friends or colleagues and would like to be able to appreciate the culture more. If you want to renew, relearn, and refresh the Spanish in your head, you'll be happy to know that puzzles and word games are a fun and effective way to do just that.

Tackling a New Language: It's Never Too Late

The best time to learn a new language is right now! In fact, the most important thing you inherit as a member of the human race is the innate capacity to learn language. Each of us learns at least one during our lifetime, and some of us want to learn more than one.

Knowing another language enables you to see the world through the eyes of the speakers of that language, and they do see it differently. When you can grasp and appreciate others' understanding of the world, you can get out there and engage with all those other fascinating people and be receptive and ready to enrich your life experience.

Language is humankind's greatest invention. It's so much more than grammatical rules and vocabulary; it's a window through which you can view the values and perspectives of the people who speak the language, and it's a mirror that reflects our common cultural heritage and humanity.

Figuring out something new doesn't have to be drudgery. Puzzles and word games offer you the chance to have some fun while you progress through your Spanish education (or any other education, for that matter). Mastering a language doesn't have to be dry, boring, and intimidating. If it's fun and recreational, it doesn't feel like work, and you remember your newfound knowledge better!

Expanding the Language Centers of Your Brain

When you exercise your body, it gets stronger, healthier, and more flexible. The same is true for your brain. The upcoming sections explain what happens when you exercise your brain.

Creating new storage files in your brain

By stimulating and exercising the parts of your brain that process language, you create new storage space where you can stash Spanish words and phrases. In other words, studying another language makes you smarter because it increases your brain capacity! This "brain remodeling" opens up your memory space and benefits *all* linguistic output; as you work on your Spanish, you liven up and clarify your English at the same time.

The best way to understand fully your own language is to study someone else's. No wonder schools have foreign language requirements!

Sharpening your memory along with your pencil

Puzzles give you a fun outlet to practice and reinforce your language talents. Practice is the most beneficial way to get all that information to stick in your memory. The more you practice, the better your memory gets!

Some of the puzzles in this book include only Spanish words, which gives you the opportunity to think in the target language and to become more comfortable with the new spelling combinations and structures that you need to absorb to become fluent. As you solve these Spanish-only puzzles, you reinforce new spelling patterns and sequences. (And spelling in Spanish is *much* easier than spelling in English!)

Many of the puzzles and games ask you to translate from one language to the other, which improves and develops your dictionary skills. Before you know it, your English vocabulary increases because you have absorbed Spanish words with similar spellings and nearly identical meanings. (For English speakers, Spanish is an ideal first foreign language to learn because of the huge number of corresponding words, which provides an immediate sense of success and understanding for the learner.)

Translation is an extremely important tool for acquiring vocabulary and for making you feel confident and successful. However, translation also reinforces the idea that language is just words and gives a false impression that absolutely everything has exact linguistic equivalents. To really grasp a language, you have to become comfortable with how it works as a whole, inside and outside of everyday environments, instead of expecting it to mirror your own language. We set up this book with thematic chapters to give you those realistic contexts and situations so you can remember the vocabulary more easily and logically.

In some cases, a puzzle or game furthers your Spanish studies simply by exposing you to spelling, subject matter, names, or cultural items. We hope that finding a new word or name piques your interest, and that you're inspired to find out more about that particular item.

The more context you can associate with your newfound knowledge, the better you're able to remember and appreciate what you've acquired. Connect the names, themes, or cultural tidbits with the vocabulary you're studying, and you get a mental picture that won't disappear from your memory anytime soon.

Building Vocabulary the Easy Way

This book doesn't just throw a bunch of words and phrases at you in a haphazard fashion. We present Spanish vocabulary in a thematic way, with logical categories and context. These themes echo basic

Spanish courses, textbooks, and phrase books. Each chapter is dedicated to a particular theme, and we created a variety of different puzzles for each chapter, so you get a diversified linguistic workout. You don't have the drudgery of dealing with huge word lists with these puzzles; instead, you have the pleasure of getting the vocabulary in little bites rather than huge, overwhelming gulps.

Puzzles and word games tickle the visual and the intellectual sides of your brain. Some of the games in this book are very visually oriented; others require more systematic and deliberate approaches. All of them provide you with a quick, delightful way to practice and an immediate sense of satisfaction and achievement. In every case, you are exposed to as much Spanish as befits the type of puzzle.

Achieving Success Inside or Outside the Classroom

As you go through the puzzles, keep in mind *las tres palabras claves* (the three key words): *práctica, perseverancia,* and *paciencia.* These are, in order of importance:

- ✔ **Practice** creates all that new brain storage space and stimulates even more learning.

- ✔ **Perseverance** keeps the acquisition and motivation processes going strong.

- ✔ **Patience** keeps you focused on your goal for taking up Spanish in the first place, whether it's getting a better grade in class; being able to converse effectively with the natives during your dream vacation to South America; or initiating, reliving, and appreciating an engaging memory with a Spanish speaker (and maybe bringing new meaning to the term *Romance language*).

Buena suerte. . .¡y al toro!

Chapter 2

Taking the Puzzlement out of Puzzles

*Y*ou may not be aware of this, but you're surrounded by puzzles, even if they don't look like those you might traditionally find in a magazine or newspaper. Some can be quite pleasant, such as deciding on the perfect birthday gift to give someone or adjusting measurements in the recipe for your favorite dessert. Others are considerably less enjoyable, such as trying to find your lost car keys or filing your income taxes — and boy, is *that* a puzzle!

Although the puzzles in this book come in a variety of shapes and sizes, they all have the same goal: to help you improve your Spanish language skills in an entertaining way. In this chapter, we review the major puzzle types that appear in Part II and provide helpful strategies to help you improve your solving skills, which in turn, improve your language skills.

 Some of the tips and suggestions for solving the puzzles in this book are unique to the Spanish language, such as optimal solving strategies based on letter patterns. Although some suggestions may apply to more than one puzzle type, we include each under the heading where it is likely to be the most useful.

Thinking inside the Box with Crosswords

The crossword puzzles in this book may not look quite like the ones you're used to. The crosswords in your daily newspaper are usually referred to as *Standard American* puzzles, and they have several properties:

- ✔ All the words appear in a square grid — usually 15x15 or 21x21, although they sometimes vary.

- ✔ There are no *unchecked letters*. That is, every letter must be part of two words — one that goes across and another that goes down.

- ✔ They contain *rotational symmetry* — if you turn the puzzle upside down or rotate it 180 degrees, the grid still looks the same.

- ✔ Many puzzles contain a theme. This means that there are usually several words or multiword entries that relate to each other in some way. Depending on the size of the puzzle, the nature of the theme, and the ability of the constructor to interlock the entries, theme entries might occupy as much as one-third of the overall letter count.

- ✔ They contain no two-letter words.

Most Spanish crossword puzzles — such as the ones in Spanish-language newspapers — lack several of these properties. Some letters appear in words that go in only one direction. Black squares aren't necessarily placed in a symmetrical pattern. Puzzles may contain two-letter words.

To get around these issues we decided to construct crosswords in a style of puzzle that is sometimes referred to as *student, free-form, criss-cross,* or *vocabulary*. We like the term *vocabulary puzzle* best, because what the puzzles may lack in symmetry or aesthetics, they make up for by having *all* of their entries related to the theme. For a language student, this kind of dedication to theme enables you to focus your energies on the words around a specific topic.

Most of the crosswords in this book involve some form of English-to-Spanish translation, although occasional puzzles involve Spanish-to-English translation. The clues are English or Spanish words, and your job is to enter their translations in Spanish or English, respectively, in the grid. Every word is connected to at least one other word by at least one letter. But you're working out more than your translation muscles — you're also getting valuable practice with writing and with recognizing the sound patterns and letter clusters in Spanish.

Much of the advice on how to solve crossword puzzles you might encounter in books refers to Standard American puzzles. Here are a few suggestions that may be particularly useful for the vocabulary puzzles in this book:

✔ **Start with entries you know.** Even if you review all the clues and recognize only one that you know, you're off to a good start. Enter that word in the grid. You've already gained valuable hints as to the letter positions of the connecting words.

✔ **Use letters in words that are already filled in as clues.** Sometimes you might have trouble visualizing the word in the crossword grid itself. Try writing out the word elsewhere on the page, as if you were playing hangman. Looking at the pattern of letters and blanks may help you think of other words that fit this particular pattern and relate to the theme.

✔ **Look for plurals.** Unlike English, which has many irregular plurals, such as *cacti* or *teeth,* all Spanish plurals end in S. (S if the singular ends in a vowel, ES if it ends in a consonant.) So if a clue word refers to a plural, you're fairly safe to put an S in the last position.

✔ **Remember the theme.** Because all of the crosswords in Part II are thematic, you may know some members of a particular category even if you don't know their translations. For example, if you're solving a crossword about animals, make a list of all the animals you can think of in the language to which you are translating, and then see whether any of the clues correspond to what you've written. This tip might be particularly useful for solving the crosswords in this book, because you might be stuck on a word even if you have filled in all the other words with which it intersects.

✔ **Think of related words in other languages you might already know.** You may also find connections to other information in your knowledge base. In the case of Spanish, words are often similar to those in other Romance languages. You may recognize *pollo* is the word for *chicken* either from knowing that it happens to be the same word in Italian or that it's derived from the same root as the English word *poultry.*

Filling in the Blanks of Fill-Ins

Fill-ins are a variety of crossword puzzle without numbers in the grid. The clues are listed according to word length, and part of your job is figuring out where the words fit so that all the answers interlock. A particular word may fit in more than one location, but the overall solution to the puzzle is unique.

The word lengths for the fill-ins in this book refer to the lengths of the words after you translate them from English to Spanish or vice versa. For example, TREE would appear under the heading "5 Letters" because the Spanish word for *tree* is *árbol.*

Quite a few of the strategies for solving fill-ins are similar to those for crosswords. Start by making a list of all the words you can think of that relate to the theme in the language to which you are translating (English or Spanish); some of them may be on the word list. You can also try to guess some of the words from their roots.

The following approaches are unique to solving fill-ins:

- ✔ **Look at the word list.** Notice the lengths of the words in the list. For example, if only one word appears under the heading "7 Letters," then the grid contains only one corresponding space for a seven-letter word, and so you already know where that word fits in the grid. Filling in words that fit in only one spot is definitely the best place to start regardless of how many words you might know.

- ✔ **Go to extremes.** If no words of unique lengths appear in a particular puzzle, start with the shortest and the longest words on the list. The shorter words are likely to intersect with fewer other words, which narrows down the possibilities for words with which they might intersect. Shorter words are also likely to be more common.

  On the other hand, you may find that longer words, when placed, give more hints to finding connecting words so that you have more opportunities to work with. Longer entries are less common, but a number of them have helpful tags, such as "(2 words)" or "(3 words)" if they are multiword phrases.

- ✔ **Look for clues by word length and letters you've already placed.** After you place a few words in the grid, notice the lengths of the intersecting words as well as the letters you filled in and their positions.

  For example, if a word in the grid crosses a six-letter word with an R in the fourth position, look at the six-letter words in your lists and see which ones have an R in the fourth position. If only one word meets those criteria, then you know that the word belongs at that crossing. If the list contains more than one six-letter word with the R in the fourth position, then you need to try them, one at a time, looking at additional interlocks. This process involves trial and error, and some element of logical deduction, but you'll feel an enormous sense of satisfaction upon seeing the completed grid.

Navigating Word Searches

The word searches in this book show up in a slew of special presentations. Some appear in grids that form an image related to the theme. In others, the leftover letters spell an appropriate word or phrase.

In addition to those that involve translation of word lists from English to Spanish and vice versa, we include a few word searches in which both the word lists and the grids are in Spanish. We include these in cases where the puzzle theme generated a very long word list with relatively few *cognates* (words that have a common etymological origin) that would otherwise help you translate them. Even though these puzzles don't require translation, they do strengthen your knowledge of basic pattern recognition and reinforce Spanish spelling patterns.

Seek & find

Most of the word search puzzles in this book are the type that you're probably most familiar with, which we're calling *seek & find*.

Words in a seek & find puzzle run in every possible direction: vertically, horizontally, and diagonally.

After you discover at least one word to look for in the grid, try one or any combination of these approaches:

- ✔ **Start at the beginning.** One of the most efficient techniques is to scan all the rows and columns for the first letter of the word you are looking for. For example, if you are looking for the word BOSQUE (forest), you first look for a B in the grid. From there, you look at the letters adjacent to the B and look for an O. (Depending on where you find the B, you may have as many as eight other letters to scan.) After you find a BO cluster, look for an S adjacent to the O, and so on until the word BOSQUE reveals itself.

- ✔ **Look for letters with unique shapes or features.** Another approach to looking for the word BOSQUE is to start looking for the letter Q, because its tail is a property not shared by any other letter. (Of course, the Q is also a good place to start because if it has no U adjacent to it, it's probably not part of any word.) Other letters with properties that may "pop out" are J (with its hook shape), X (with its cross), and — unique to Spanish — Ñ, with its *tilde*.

- ✔ **Assess letter frequency.** Besides having certain shapes that differ from traditional lines and curves, some letters may be more noticeable because of their relative rarity. Letters that appear less frequently might be easier to spot by mere nature of their novelty. Letter frequency is sometimes hard to assess because language changes all the time; the letter W, for instance, which is extremely rare in Spanish, may become more common over time, because of its use in Internet terms such as *Web*. Still, it's unlikely to surpass E as the most common letter in Spanish.

The five most common letters in Spanish are E, A, O, S, and R. These five letters account for slightly less than half of all the letters in Spanish based on frequency analysis. The five least common are Z, Ñ, X, W, and K. Start by looking for the rarer letters in the list.

✔ **The more words you find, the easier the puzzle gets.** Starting a word search can be daunting; you're staring at an array of letters that has yet to be whittled. Take heart in knowing that the more words you circle, the less open space there is in the grid. And the less open space you have, the easier the remaining words are to find.

Secret lists

In secret list word searches, we don't give you a list of words to find but tell you how many words related to the theme you need to look for in the grid. In all the secret list word search puzzles in this book, we give you instructions in English, and you hunt for Spanish words in the grid.

You can use the strategies described for seek & find puzzles, and here are some additional tips that are unique to secret list word searches:

✔ **Think of elements in the theme that you might already know.** For example, if the instructions read: "Twenty words for colors appear in this grid. Can you find them all?" you might start out by thinking of all the words for colors you already know or think you know, or might recognize by their cognates, and then look for them in the grid. For example, if you didn't know that *azul* was the Spanish word for *blue,* you might think of synonyms for *blue* that are similar to *azul,* such as *azure.*

✔ **Write down your answers.** Even though you might be able to head straight for the grid and keep track of multiple words in your memory, writing them down — or even saying them aloud — strengthens the connections in your brain that help you remember the words' spellings and meanings.

✔ **Pay attention to word length.** To help you keep track of the words you find, we provide spaces below the grid, grouped by word length. Write in the words you find, and then you won't be tempted to look for them again. More importantly, you can note the lengths of the words in the grid that you haven't yet found, based on the spaces still open. If, for example, you have one word left to find, knowing its length provides a good clue about what word you're looking for.

Unscrambling Word Scrambles

If you're like us and admire the fact that the letters in the French phrase *la mer* ("the sea") can be rearranged to form the Spanish phrase *el mar,* which also means "the sea," you probably enjoy scramble puzzles.

For all of the scrambles in this book, we ask you to rearrange strings of letters to form Spanish words related to the theme of the puzzle. As a warm-up, we list the shorter — and therefore easier to unscramble — words earlier in the puzzle. Several puzzles involve some variation, but you can solve all of them better by following these tips:

✔ **Know your Spanish letter patterns.** We could spend several chapters going over all the rules of Spanish spelling and word formation, but here we stick to key points that guide you through some of the other hints in this section.

As you work through the scrambles, the following facts about Spanish spelling may help:

- Spanish is spelled exactly as it is pronounced, except for the letter H, which is silent unless it follows a C to form a *ch* sound.

- Most Spanish words alternate consonants and vowels, and most syllables start with consonants.

- Two-letter consonant clusters (such as FL and TR) are much less common in Spanish than in English; three-letter consonant clusters (such as STR and SCR) are comparatively rare.

- Except for LL and RR, double letters are uncommon, except occasionally for CC and, less commonly, NN.

✔ **Look beyond the page.** If you're looking at a letter sequence such as IMAGO and find yourself staring into space, unable to see the word AMIGO, try using some other tools. If you have a set of Scrabble tiles or Boggle cubes or a copy of the old game Anagrams, you can take out the letters that match those in the puzzle and rearrange them. If you don't have any of these games at home, you can write the letters out on index cards or slips of paper and use those.

Sometimes rearranging the letters physically is a lot easier than doing so mentally. Anything that helps you look at the letters differently is useful and can move you toward the correct answer.

✔ **Rewrite the letters in new arrangements.** We stress throughout this part of the book the importance of writing as a means
to help reinforce Spanish spelling patterns, and here's a perfect
opportunity to use this strategy. In addition to writing out other
permutations of letters of IMAGO such as MOGIA or OGIMA, try
alternating consonants and vowels. (Most Spanish words follow
this pattern.) Another common technique is to write the letters
in an array other than a straight line — try a circle, wavelike
pattern, or any other shape.

Visualizing the letters in different patterns and using multiple
sensory pathways improves not only your puzzle solving but
also your language-learning skills.

Cracking the Cryptogram Code

When Adam recently visited the National Cryptologic Museum, he
was amazed at the rooms of supercomputers that were once used
to perform billions of computations to help crack codes during
wartime. The cryptograms in this book aren't nearly as complicated
as those old security codes, but they are probably the hardest
puzzles in this book. Don't worry, though: the human brain is
quite a powerful machine and can do a lot of things that even the
smartest computers can't.

The cryptograms in this book are grouped as lists of coded Spanish
words and phrases that relate to the theme of the puzzle.

Every letter in a cryptogram is coded to represent a different letter
of the alphabet. Because Spanish has an extra letter — Ñ — none
of the words in the cryptograms contains that letter.

Although the lists are not *pangrams* — that is, they don't necessarily contain all the letters of the alphabet — all of the letters that *do*
appear in the puzzle appear at least twice, in two different words.
This means that you won't find yourself in a situation where the entire
puzzle is solved except for one pesky letter that you can't figure out!

We also provide various hints to get you started (we sometimes
give you the article with the word, so when you see a two-letter
combination of L with E or A, try using the articles EL and LA), and
we decode the first word in the list as an example.

The same code applies for all the words throughout a puzzle. For
example, if X becomes E in one word, it does so for all the words in
that particular puzzle (but not necessarily for all the cryptogram
puzzles in the book). Here are some other strategies that help you
decode cryptograms:

✔ **Start at the end.** Sounds weird, huh? Depending on the types of words that are in the list, you often get valuable information from the last letters in the words. If all the letters at the end of the words are the same, they might all be plurals, which would make them Ss; verb infinitives, which would mean they are Rs; or adjectives, in which case it's a good bet that they are Os.

Although Spanish adjectives agree in both gender and number with their corresponding nouns, in this book, unless otherwise specified, we use the common default form in Spanish, which is the singular masculine ending of O.

✔ **Let the Spanish language guide you.** You can use some of the other information about Spanish spelling patterns we discuss in the section "Unscrambling Word Scrambles." For example, given a sequence such as ZZEREH, the double letters at the beginning have to be LL because no other double-letter combinations are possible at the beginning of a word; the two Es must be vowels and could be either A or O, so the word could be LLAMAR or LLOROS. Of course, this example is in isolation; you would also be able to use hints from the other words in the list to help narrow down your possibilities.

Spicing Up Your Life with Variety Puzzles

Because new experiences are terrific stimulation for the brain, we include some puzzles that look a little different from those in the major puzzle categories we describe in the previous sections. Some might be similar with relatively minor alterations, but some might be completely new and different. (In particular, all the challenge puzzles in Chapter 11 are different in one way or another; some are totally new puzzle types, and others are hybrid puzzles that combine elements of two or more of the major puzzle types.)

Don't be intimidated by such variety; try to approach these new puzzles in the same way you would trying a food for the first time. Just because a puzzle is new or different, it isn't necessarily more difficult.

To help you approach these challenges, we provide extra information in the introductions to guide you along. Depending on the puzzle, some of the solving strategies in this chapter may be useful; feel free to come back to this chapter any time you need to review those techniques.

Further Tips and Suggestions

Here are a few tips and suggestions for puzzle-solving in general. These are not unique to any particular puzzle type and can be applied to puzzles in any language. Here goes:

✔ **Read the title and instructions.** We could have given very straightforward titles to the puzzles, but that wouldn't be very exciting, would it? While the titles usually involve some form of pun or wordplay, they're designed to exercise your mind from the get-go, without being misleading.

Reading the instructions is not a method of last resort but a good idea from the start. Even if you see a crossword grid or a list of letter strings that looks like a cryptogram, you may be in for twists or other novelties that require you to approach the puzzle in a different way. The instructions let you know what to expect.

✔ **Use a pencil, or a pen with an eraser.** You might be surprised to know that some participants in various puzzle competitions that we attend, such as the American Crossword Puzzle Tournament, prefer to use pen over pencil because the ink of the pen runs smoother on paper than the graphite of the pencil, and in a contest of speed, even a sliver of time makes a difference. Even so, we don't know anyone, no matter how skilled, who would feel comfortable without at least using a pen with an eraser.

Some of the puzzles in this book are harder than others, and some require trying multiple possibilities before you reach the correct answer. You might even make some mistakes here and there; it happens to even the best solvers. Sometimes, erasing an answer that you think may be wrong frees your mind to approach the puzzle with a clean slate that enables you to consider other options, one of which might be correct.

✔ **Use reference materials.** Some people think that they're cheating if they look up words in a dictionary, search for answers on the Internet, or ask a friend for assistance. We think you should use whatever tools you have at your disposal if doing so improves your enjoyment of the solving experience. In fact, because the puzzles in this book are designed to be educational as well as fun, we actually encourage you to look up things that you might not know; the research itself helps further instill the information in your memory. Similarly, if you don't need help while actually solving a puzzle, something in that particular puzzle might catch your interest and spark your curiosity to do further research about that topic on your own.

✔ **Find a solving partner.** Solving puzzles tends to be a solitary activity. Not unlike a study group you might have formed back in school, co-solving a puzzle allows you to bounce ideas back and forth with your partner, perhaps filling in gaps in each other's knowledge, and also reinforces the educational component of the puzzles. A solving buddy is also likely to make the experience much more fun.

✔ **Take a break if you get stuck.** Sometimes, just putting a puzzle down and refocusing your mind on another activity — taking a walk, calling a friend, or seeing a movie, for example — can help you approach the puzzle in a fresh way when you return. Whether or not you found the answer to the puzzle on your walk, with your friend, or at the theater, sometimes all you need is a little break to look at the puzzle from a new perspective.

✔ **Don't give up!** We get really upset when we sometimes hear people say "Oh, I'm not smart enough to do puzzles!" Puzzles are not intelligence tests; they merely present a snapshot of a particular set of information or challenge at a particular time.

Keep in mind the three key words from Chapter 1: *practice, perseverance,* and *patience.* Becoming fluent in a language or becoming an expert puzzle solver (or just about anything else) requires repetition and dedication. A particularly tough challenge may frustrate you, but keep at it! We hope that the strategies we discuss in this chapter, with the initiative you've already shown by picking up this book and reading this far, minimize any frustration you may have and maximize your educational benefit and enjoyment.

Part II
The Puzzles

The 5th Wave   By Rich Tennant

"No wrong answers – please! Not easy
make erasures."

In this part...

Now you're in for the fun of it! Each chapter in this part is dedicated to a particular theme, the kinds you find in today's textbooks, to keep the vocabulary focused. But if you're not using a textbook, you still find plenty here to fill your needs vocabulary-wise, and to pique your puzzle interest because of the many varieties packed into this part of the book.

Chapter 3

Everyday Words and Phrases

Puzzle 1: Opening Lines

Unscramble the words below to form a short conversation between Diego and Susana. The English translations are in parentheses.

1. LOHA. ¿OMÓC TESÁS? (Hello, how are you?)

2. YMU IBNE, SAGRIAC. ¿Y ÚT? (Very well, thanks. And you?)

3. TABANSET NIBE, CIGARAS. (Quite well, thank you.)

4. YOS GIODE. ¿MOÓC ET SALMAL? (I'm Diego. What's your name?)

5. EM MALOL NASSAU. (My name is Susana.)

6. ANECDOTAN, AUSANS. (Very nice to meet you, Susana.)

7. CHOMU STOGU, EDOGI. (It's a pleasure, Diego.)

8. ¿ED NÓDED SEER, ASUNAS? (Where are you from, Susana?)

9. SYO ED VUANE KYRO. ¿Y ÚT? (I'm from New York. And you?)

10. OSY ED FILCANIORA. (I'm from California.)

11. ¿EDÓDNA SAV OHARA? (Where are you going now?)

12. VYO LA NICE. ¿Y ÚT? (To the movies. And you?)

13. OVY LA CREMODA. (I'm going to the market.)

14. NUOBE, ¡SON EVOMS RONTOP! (Okay, see you soon!)

15. SUPE, ¡SHATA ULOGE, IDEGO! (Well, later, Diego!)

16. SÓDIA, SAUNAS. (Good-bye, Susana.)

Puzzle 2: Time Management

Translate the time-related words below from English to Spanish and enter them into the grid. More than one word may fill any particular space, but the overall solution is unique.

Hint: The words are grouped by the number of letters in their Spanish translation. Don't include articles in the translations.

3 Letters
DAY
MONTH
TODAY
YEAR

4 Letters
HOUR
MAY
YESTERDAY

5 Letters
AFTERNOON
APRIL
AUTUMN
CENTURY
DATE
EVENING
JANUARY
JULY
JUNE
MARCH
MONDAY

6 Letters
AUGUST
DECADE
MINUTE
MORNING/TOMORROW
SATURDAY
SUMMER
THURSDAY
TUESDAY
WEEK

7 Letters
FEBRUARY
OCTOBER
SECOND
SUNDAY
FRIDAY

8 Letters
WINTER

9 Letters
DECEMBER
NOVEMBER
SPRING
WEDNESDAY

10 Letters
CALENDAR
SEPTEMBER

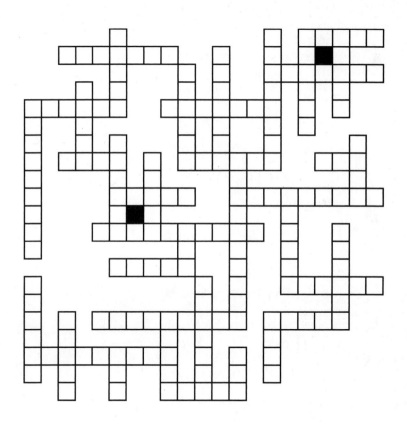

Puzzle 3: On Holiday

This crossword commemorates various holidays and observances celebrated throughout the United States and the Spanish-speaking world. Translate the English names in the clues into Spanish and insert them into the grid. After you complete the puzzle, go ahead and celebrate!

Hint: The Day of the Dead is a version of All Soul's Day celebrated in Mexico and other Spanish-speaking countries.

Across

4 GOOD FRIDAY (2 words)

7 HOLY WEEK (2 words)

8 THANKSGIVING (5 words)

10 NEW YEAR'S DAY (2 words)

13 MARDI GRAS

15 EPIPHANY

16 ALL SOUL'S DAY (4 words)

17 CHANUKAH

18 ALL SAINT'S DAY (3 words)

Down

1 LENT

2 DAY OF THE DEAD (4 words)

3 NEW YEAR'S EVE

5 CHRISTMAS

6 EASTER (2 words)

9 PALM SUNDAY (3 words)

11 CHRISTMAS EVE

12 EID (END OF RAMADAN)

14 PASSOVER

Puzzle 4: Twenty Questions

Knowing all the answers is great, but sometimes you don't even know all the questions. Twenty question words and phrases hide in this word search grid, some more than once. To figure out which ones are hidden, and with what frequency, insert a question word into each of these sentences to form a grammatically correct question. More than one word may work for a particular question, but after you complete the puzzle correctly, you have a one-to-one match between the words circled and those written in the sentences.

1. ¿ _____ HORA ES?

2. ¿ _____ TE LLAMAS?

3. ¿ _____ SABE?

4. ¿ _____ AÑOS TIENE?

5. ¿ _____ ES LA FECHA DE HOY?

6. ¿ _____ ES TU DÍA DE CUMPLEAÑOS?

7. ¿ _____ ESTUDIAS EL ESPAÑOL?

8. ¿ _____ HAY DE NUEVO?

9. ¿ _____ ESTÁ EL CUARTO DE BAÑO?

10. ¿ _____ ES TU NÚMERO DE TELÉFONO?

11. ¿ DE _____ ERES?

12. ¿ _____ ESTÁ USTED?

13. ¿ _____ QUIERE DECIR?

14. ¿ _____ SON TUS AMIGOS?

15. ¿ _____ TIEMPO HACE?

16. ¿ _____ CHICAS HAY EN LA FAMILIA?

17. ¿ _____ NO TIENES EL DINERO?

18. ¿ _____ ES LA CAPITAL DE COLOMBIA?

19. ¿ _____ VAS EL LUNES?

20. ¿ _____ TE GRADÚAS DE LA UNIVERSIDAD?

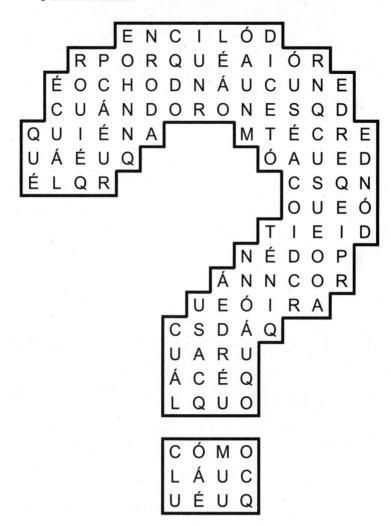

Puzzle 5: Color Coding

Below you find a list of coded Spanish names for colors. Can you decode the items in Spanish? Ignore accent marks, and the letter Ñ does not appear in any of the answers. We've given you the first entry as a hint to get you started.

Hint: Colors, like all adjectives, agree with the nouns they modify, but all the answers here take the singular masculine form.

1. SKMCU = NEGRO (BLACK)

2. TJTCOEEU

3. TSTCTSLTIU

4. JTCCUS

5. CULU

6. WETSXU

7. BKCIK

8. WCUSXKTIU

9. TQYE

10. CUVTIU

11. WETSXYQXU

12. MCOV

13. JUCTIU

14. IUCTIU

15. ETBTSIT

~~BLACK~~	GRAY	PINK
BLUE	GREEN	PURPLE
BRONZE	LAVENDER	RED
BROWN	OFF-WHITE	WHITE
GOLD	ORANGE	YELLOW

Puzzle 6: Exclamation Points

Wow! Translate these 15 English exclamations into Spanish, and find their equivalents in the grid. After you find them all, the remaining letters spell out, in order, an exclamation that is also the title of a song from the 2008 Tony award winner for Best Musical, *In the Heights*.

```
D  I  O  S  M  Í  O  N  E
S  A  V  É  U  Q  O  M  Y
O  Q  U  É  P  E  N  A  O
I  B  E  F  U  E  G  O  P
D  A  R  R  I  B  A  S  O
R  S  O  M  A  V  D  A  R
O  T  N  E  I  S  O  L  F
P  A  I  V  G  R  A  U  I
Í  M  E  D  Y  A  A  D  N
```

DEAR ME!/OH MY GOSH!

ENOUGH!

FINALLY!/AT LAST!

FIRE!

FOR GOODNESS SAKE!

GESUNDHEIT!/CHEERS!

HOORAY! (2 entries)

I'M SORRY!

LET'S GO!

LISTEN!/HEY!

LOOK!

NO WAY!/YOU'RE KIDDING!

WHAT A PITY!

WOE IS ME!

Puzzle 7: Summing Up

Rearrange each word string below to form a number in Spanish. When you've correctly unscrambled all the words, add their values. The sum is equal to a year in Spanish history well-known for a famous excursion. What is the year and what was the event?

SOD	_____ +	CINQUE	_____ +
LMI	_____ +	RUTOCA	_____ +
NOU	_____ +	INVEET	_____ +
NICE	_____ +	NITRATE	_____ +
REST	_____ +	TEROCCA	_____ +
CODE	_____ +	TRUECANA	_____ +
CONE	_____ +	UNIACCENT	_____ +
ZIDE	_____ +	SÉCIEDISI	_____ +
COOH	_____ +	COCHEIDIO	_____ +
ESSI	_____ +	VENICEIDUE	_____ +
CRETE	_____ +	IDISIECETE	_____ +
VENUE	_____ +	ASSENTE Y OSD	_____ =
OCCIN	_____ +	*Sum*	_____
EITES	_____ +		

What famous excursion took place this year?

Puzzle 8: Hide and Seek

In this game of hide and seek, we ask you to look for opposites, this time playing with verb infinitives. If we give you HIDE, for example, you have to find its antonym, SEEK.

```
T E S R A T N A V E L R
O R A T S A G L R R R I
M U A E M P O S A E Q L
A R P R B O L U R D U A
R L A M R N L B A N I S
E R G I L E F I P E T R
R A A N D R C R E V A A
P L R A M O J A R H R R
R E D R E P P R R C S O
E M P L E A R T A E E L
V M O R I R I N E V R L
E E S R A T R E P S E D
```

ABRIR	DAR	ROMPER
ACOSTARSE	DESPEDIR	SACAR
AHORRAR	ENCENDER	SALIR
AMAR	ENCONTRAR	SECAR
BAJAR	IR	SENTARSE
COMENZAR/EMPEZAR	PONERSE	VIVIR
COMPRAR	REÍR	

Puzzle 9: Opposites Attract

For better or worse, here's hoping you have no ease, er, difficulty, with this puzzle. In this crossword, all the correct entries in the grid are the opposites of their corresponding clues.

Across

2 BAJO (short in height)

4 AHORA (now)

6 DIFERENTE (different)

8 PELIGROSO (dangerous)

9 POBRE (poor)

11 BONITO (pretty)

12 ANTIPÁTICO (unfriendly)

14 LENTO/DESPACIO (slow)

15 TARDE (late)

17 FRÍO (cold)

20 DIFÍCIL (difficult)

23 SIN (without)

24 CORTO (short in length)

25 NEGATIVO (negative)

29 DETRÁS (in back of)

30 LIGERO (lightweight)

Down

1 CERCA (near)

2 CERRADO (closed)

3 MALO (bad)

5 MUERTO (dead)

7 ABAJO (down)

10 OSCURO (dark)

11 TRISTE (sad)

13 TONTO (dumb)

16 MENOR (younger)

17 BARATO (cheap)

18 BLANCO (white)

19 GORDO (fat)

21 SUCIO (dirty)

22 PEQUEÑO (small)

25 DESPUÉS (afterward)

26 PEOR (worse)

27 JOVEN (young)

Puzzle 10: A Time and Place for Everything

Translate these Spanish words for prepositions, which are grouped according to the number of letters in their English equivalents. More than one word may fit in a particular space, but the overall solution is unique.

Hint: Although A and EN can refer to two different answers in the grid, one word is common to both of them.

2 Letters
A (2 entries)
DE
EN (2 entries)

4 Letters
CON
DE
SOBRE

5 Letters
ARRIBA
DESPUÉS DE/TRAS

6 Letters
AL LADO DE/PRÓXIMO A
   (2 words)
ALREDEDOR DE
ANTES DE
A TRAVÉS DE
CERCA DE (2 words)
DENTRO DE
DETRÁS DE
HACIA

7 Letters
ENCIMA DE (3 words)
ENTRE
FUERA DE
POR
SIN

9 Letters
A LA IZQUIERDA (3 words)
DELANTE DE/ENFRENTE DE
   (3 words)

10 Letters
A LA DERECHA
DEBAJO DE

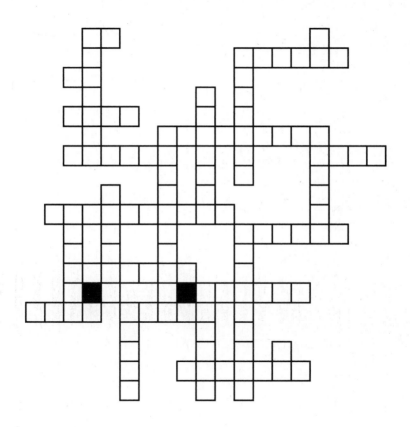

Puzzle 11: Ready for Action

Fifty of the most common Spanish verb infinitives are encoded in this cryptogram. We provide their English translations to guide you. Because you have the first answer as an example (IR for GO), you have a head start toward all the other entries in the list; all the answers end in the letter R.

1. EQ = IR

2. CXQ

3. YEQ

4. IFQ

5. UFFQ

6. XLQEQ

7. LFLFQ

8. AXLFQ

9. AYWFQ

10. AQFFQ

11. CFAEQ

12. PXAFQ

13. GZOXQ

14. WEQXQ

15. KXOXQ

16. KYCFQ

17. KYBFQ

18. RXLFQ

19. RXUEQ

20. JFBFQ

21. JYWXQ

22. JQXFQ

23. IEIEQ

24. AFQQXQ

25. AYBJXQ

26. CFRFXQ

27. CYQWEQ

28. PXLUXQ

29. KFBRXQ

30. KFQCFQ

31. IFBCFQ

32. IEXGXQ

33. AXWLEXQ

34. AYWKQXQ

35. AYBYAFQ

36. UEWKEXQ

37. XKQFBCFQ

38. AYWFBMXQ

39. FRAQELEQ

40. FRAZAPXQ

41. FRJZCEXQ

42. EBJFBJXQ

43. KFQWEJEQ

44. JFQWEBXQ

45. ZJEUEMXQ

46. FBAYBJQXQ

47. BFAFREJXQ

48. KQFOZBJXQ

49. QFRKYBCFQ

50. AYWKQFBCFQ

ALLOW	~~GO~~	SAY/TELL
ANSWER	HAVE	SEE
ASK	HEAR	SELL
BE ABLE	KNOW (BE ACQUAINTED WITH)	SLEEP
BEGIN/START	KNOW (FACTS)/KNOW HOW	SPEAK
BRING	LEARN	STUDY
BUY	LEAVE	TAKE
CHANGE/EXCHANGE	LISTEN	TELL/RELATE
CLEAN	LIVE	THINK (2 entries)
CLOSE	LOOK	TRAVEL
DO/MAKE	LOSE	TRY/INTEND
DRINK	NEED	UNDERSTAND/ COMPREHEND
EAT	OPEN	USE
END	PAY	WANT/DESIRE
FIND	PLAY (A GAME)	WRITE
FIT	PUT	
GIVE	READ	

Puzzle 12: Lost in Translation

Whether you're a native Spanish speaker, studying the language in a classroom, or reading *Spanish For Dummies,* you've likely encountered many terms related to language and language learning. Can you find 38 of them in this word search grid?

Hint: Many of the clue words are cognates, which should make recognizing them easier.

```
O A P Z I T A M S U S T A N T I V O R
R D R A O T I R C S E O T N E C A O O
E E E I R A N E O E O P A S A D O R L
N F S C U E I A Z M S L C U P O D E U
É I E N T R G Z A O S A R O G Z A M C
G N N A U B O O A V C I R I X N G Ú Í
H I T D F M N R D I H E D F E R E N T
T C E R P O I A V T O L L O A C Ó L R
I I D O B N N C E E Ñ A U M M I E T A
E Ó L C B O I I R J E P Á L C O R I U
M N I N M R M Ó B D A T N A C A S N M
P A T O E P E N I A I B G R D O I F A
O N O C T H F V O C A U A U S Í N I S
V C L Á U S U L A T J O C L T U G N C
E D I A L E C T O N E C B P Í P U I U
R É N F A S I S O H I J A J X S L T L
B C O N J U N C I Ó N Ñ U S E P A I I
A O D A C I F I N G I S O S E T R V N
L R N Ó I C I S O P E R P D O T O O O
```

- - - - -   - - - - - - -
- - - - -   - - - - - - -
- - - - -   - - - - - - -
- - - - -   - - - - - - -
- - - - - -   - - - - - - -
- - - - - -   - - - - - - - -
- - - - - -   - - - - - - - -
- - - - - -   - - - - - - - -
- - - - - -   - - - - - - - - -
- - - - - -   - - - - - - - - -
- - - - - -   - - - - - - - - -
- - - - - -   - - - - - - - - -
- - - - - -   - - - - - - - - -
- - - - - - -   - - - - - - - - - -
- - - - - - -   - - - - - - - - - -
- - - - - -   - - - - - - - - - -
- - - - - - -   - - - - - - - - - -
- - - - - - - -   - - - - - - - - - -
- - - - - - - -   - - - - - - - - - - -

Puzzle 13: Make Your Mark

Whether you're writing in Spanish or another language, this puzzle underscores the importance of knowing punctuation. Given the list of English words relating to written language and typography, find the Spanish translations in the grid. Note the unusual symbol in the fourth row from the bottom.

```
A E J A T N E C R O P E D O N G I S E N N
A S I D N O D E P O R A L A H C E F A Ó Ó
D U S A T C H A L U C S Ú Y A M O M P I I
I F V I S I G N O D E N Ú M E R O S U C C
T A L P F N P A R R O Ñ E S T C G Í N A A
R D M A E V A A Q U U Q L S G E R M T M G
E O I R J E Í P U E A L O H A R O B O A O
V S L É O R M I A S A P O E C A N O Y L R
N P O N R T O R C V A J D I D L E L C C R
I U C T A I N L E B E E L I G L J O O X E
A N U E G D S S O L D P É E I I S D M E T
R T A S N O A R F C A R X E T D T E A E N
R O L I E A R N R S E O T Ú S R U L A D I
A S L S Z A U U T S R N D L E A A D G O E
B C I R O C G E I A E M F A Z T O Ó E N D
G A D I R O R S X U E R R E Y S R L X G O
I H E I T I F Ó F A A R I E R A Y A A I N
L O C N S I G N O & A Y P S O B R R R S G
A L U C S Ú N I M B N U A I N N U B R I I
E P O S A L L I M O C X I R S E Q R U L S
E N N E G R I T A Y S E T E H C R O C S N
```

AMPERSAND (&)

APOSTROPHE (')

ASTERISK (*)

AT SIGN (@)

BACKSLASH (\)

BOLDFACE (**BOLDFACE)**

BRACES ({ })

BRACKETS ([ ])

CEDILLA (ç)

CIRCUMFLEX (ê)

COLON (:)

COMMA (,)

DASH (—)

DIERESIS (Ü)

DOLLAR SIGN ($)

EXCLAMATION POINT (!)

FONT (**FON**T)

ITALICS (*ITALICS*)

LETTER (L)

LOWERCASE (lowercase)

NUMBER (#)

PARENTHESIS (( ))

PAUSE (   )

PERCENTAGE SIGN (%)

PERIOD (.)

QUESTION MARK (?)

QUOTATION MARKS ("")

SEMICOLON (;)

SLASH (/)

TILDE (~)

UPPERCASE (UPPERCASE)

UPSIDE-DOWN (¡¿)

UNDERLINED (<u>UNDERLINED</u>)

Puzzle 14: Mixed Emotions

This puzzle will help you get in touch with your feelings. Unscramble the strings of letters to form adjectives in Spanish that may be used to describe someone's personal state.

Hint: Many of these adjectives end in a past participle, such as -ADO or -IDO.

1. DAMA = AMADO	16. ONTECTON
2. LEZIF	17. DÓMOCINO
3. STOLI	18. SOVERINO
4. REGALE	19. DROBAMASO
5. LOCOSE	20. DISENOVIO
6. DOCÓMO	21. QUARTLION
7. SITTER	22. DORAFATUNO
8. ODANIMA	23. DRAGADECIO
9. SODACAN	24. FUNODICOND
10. JADONEO	25. STIPEDADOS
11. TREÑOXA	26. COPREDUAPO
12. SOMEIDO	27. CHOSEPOSOS
13. DIROQUE	28. GRAVADOZONE
14. DRUBIARO	29. PRESIDOROND
15. TUSADOSA	30. LADUNISODIESO

ABSENT-MINDED	ENVIOUS	SAD
AFRAID	EXCITED	SCARED
ANGRY	FORTUNATE/LUCKY	STRANGE
ASHAMED/EMBARRASSED	GLAD	STUNNED
BELOVED	HAPPY	SURPRISED
BORED	JEALOUS	SUSPICIOUS
CALM	~~LOVED~~	THANKFUL
COMFORTABLE	NERVOUS	TIRED
CONFUSED	PLEASED	UNCOMFORTABLE
DISAPPOINTED/DISILLUSIONED	READY	WORRIED

Chapter 4

At Home

Puzzle 15: Relatively Speaking

Get the family members together for a reunion, crossword style.
Translate the English words for relatives. and place their Spanish
equivalents in the grid.

Across

2 BROTHER
5 MOTHER-IN-LAW
6 AUNT
8 UNCLE
9 GRANDMOTHER
10 WIFE
14 COUSIN (masc.)
15 NIECE
16 SON
17 FATHER-IN-LAW

Down

1 GRANDSON
2 SISTER
3 MOTHER
4 GRANDDAUGHTER
7 GRANDFATHER
10 HUSBAND
11 NEPHEW
12 COUSIN (fem.)
13 DAUGHTER
14 FATHER

Puzzle 16: Clothes Encounters

The 40 items of clothing and accessories in this puzzle run in all directions: across, down, and diagonally. Look for the plural form of those objects that generally come in pairs (like shoes), otherwise look for the singular form.

Hint: Four of the items are usually worn by men, 11 are usually worn by women, and the remaining 25 are unisex.

```
H T I R A N T E S Z A P A T I L L A S
S Z T N É L C R O P A I N T E R I O R
O A J A O T R A J E D E B A Ñ O P D S
S O M B R E R O L U Z A T E U Q A H C
B A T A N C R I T C I N T U R Ó N R D
A L D A J V O F O L E U Ñ A P A T C S
Í L U N J I T R A J Ó T B R S G A A O
M U E S A M P N B F D C I I T R L M L
A S D S A F É A L A A E M N I A O I L
Z Í O N S T U R O L T A L M E A N S I
N H T R S A C B Z D C A P A T S E E C
S Ó H O E H I O S A I E Z I N T S T N
N A S B A U N L O U R T R A N T F A O
T B G L B E Q S A M É A S A P A A Ú Z
R U E A S O P A E D J T U E J A Q L L
Í C E Q R F T A V A N G E A V R T Y A
O S É U N B B A P U A A B R I G O O C
E J A R T L N J S Q N Ó S I M A C Á S
Y E S R E J P A N T I M E D I A S E N
```

```
_ _ _ _              _ _ _ _ _ _
_ _ _ _ _            _ _ _ _ _ _
_ _ _ _ _            _ _ _ _ _ _
_ _ _ _ _            _ _ _ _ _ _ _
_ _ _ _ _            _ _ _ _ _ _ _
_ _ _ _ _            _ _ _ _ _ _ _
_ _ _ _ _            _ _ _ _ _ _ _
_ _ _ _ _ _          _ _ _ _ _ _ _
_ _ _ _ _ _          _ _ _ _ _ _ _
_ _ _ _ _ _          _ _ _ _ _ _ _
_ _ _ _ _ _          _ _ _ _ _ _ _
_ _ _ _ _ _          _ _ _ _ _ _ _
_ _ _ _ _ _          _ _ _ _ _ _ _ _
_ _ _ _ _ _          _ _ _ _ _ _ _ _ _
_ _ _ _ _ _ _        _ _ _ _ _ _ _ _ _
_ _ _ _ _ _ _        _ _ _ _ _ _ _ _ _
_ _ _ _ _ _ _        _ _ _ _ _ _ _ _ _ _
_ _ _ _ _ _ _        _ _ _ _ _ _ _ _ _ _ _
_ _ _ _ _ _ _        _ _ _ _ _ _ _ _ _ _ _
_ _ _ _ _ _ _        _ _ _ _ _ _ _ _ _ _
```

Puzzle 17: Without Further To-do

Unscramble the two columns of words below; the list on the left contains verbs related to household chores, and the list on the right contains nouns to which those chores must be performed. Match each unscrambled verb to its appropriate noun. A noun may match more than one word, but the puzzle has one unique solution.

Hint: Verbs are in infinitive form.

ACRER	~~AL AMAC~~
ADROP	LE CHECO
CRONICA	SLA TUNECAS
DICUSAR	AL PARO
GRAPA	SOL STAPOL
CHARPLAN	LE OUSEL
RIPANT	NU LEPAST
BRARRE	AL RUBASA
RAPLANE	EL PEDÉSC
LARVA	SLO SÓDIREPICO
CLICARRE	AUN STAFIE
CARROT	OLS UMBELES
RASCA	LE JEGARA
~~REACH~~	SAL STANPLA

1. MAKE THE BED   <u>HACER LA CAMA</u>

2. DUST THE FURNITURE   _____

3. IRON THE CLOTHES   _____

4. BAKE A CAKE   _____

5. MOW THE LAWN   _____

6. PAY THE BILLS   _____

7. PLAN A PARTY   _____

8. TAKE OUT THE TRASH   _____

9. RECYCLE THE NEWSPAPERS   _____

10. SWEEP THE FLOOR   _____

11. WASH THE DISHES   _____

12. TRIM THE PLANTS   _____

13. PAINT THE GARAGE   _____

14. WAX THE CAR   _____

Puzzle 18: All That Glitters

Translate the 16 jewelry-related words from English into Spanish, and then enter them into the grid. More than one word may fill any particular space, but the overall solution is unique.

Hint: The words are grouped by the number of letters in their Spanish translation. Don't include articles in the translations.

5 Letters
CHARMS
JEWELS
WATCH

6 Letters
BROOCH
CLASP
EARRINGS (STUDS)
NECKLACE
RING (BAND)

7 Letters
BRACELET
CUFFLINKS
RING (WITH
    GEMSTONE)

8 Letters
PENDANT
WEDDING RINGS

9 Letters
BANGLE BRACELET

10 Letters
EARRINGS
    (DANGLING)

16 Letters
TIE PIN (3 words)

Puzzle 19: And So to Bed

Translate the English words for items found in a bedroom and fill in the grid with their Spanish equivalents. Sweet dreams!

Across

6 NIGHTSTAND/END TABLE

7 HEADBOARD

8 CLOSET/ARMOIRE

9 SHELF

11 BLANKET

12 PILLOWCASE

16 BEDROOM

17 LAMP

18 DRAWER

19 PILLOW

Down

1 BED

2 PICTURE

3 DRESSER

4 SHEET

5 ALARM CLOCK

10 RUG

13 MATTRESS

14 BEDSPREAD

15 MIRROR

Puzzle 20: Around the House

This puzzle features a number of items around the house that you probably see every day. Can you find all of the Spanish equivalents for the household items listed in English?

```
A  I  R  E  A  C  O  N  D  I  C  I  O  N  A  D  O  C  A  O  O
Z  A  F  U  S  O  O  N  A  M  A  S  A  P  O  D  A  N  E  Ñ  B
A  Z  O  H  C  S  J  O  Á  F  Ó  B  P  E  R  S  I  A  N  A  S
R  E  H  V  U  P  U  E  R  T  A  E  Í  N  A  N  U  D  E  D  O
R  S  O  M  O  O  T  R  A  G  A  L  U  Z  I  O  Q  O  M  L  R
E  C  A  N  A  L  Ó  N  Ó  L  A  C  S  E  D  U  L  V  I  E  E
T  A  R  A  Z  R  O  P  M  I  J  S  E  L  B  E  U  M  H  P  H
O  L  J  T  É  R  Q  E  M  Ñ  E  L  U  Q  U  T  S  A  C  U  C
L  E  U  E  O  U  N  U  S  O  G  I  T  S  O  P  A  V  S  D  R
D  R  O  C  R  I  R  V  E  S  T  U  A  R  I  O  T  P  Á  E  E
O  A  L  H  A  A  U  B  O  S  I  P  A  S  I  L  L  O  I  N  P
U  E  F  O  L  B  X  Y  T  V  I  R  I  S  T  R  E  L  N  A  A
O  C  A  L  E  F  A  C  C  I  Ó  N  A  S  O  A  O  C  Í  A  A
R  T  A  A  R  R  R  Ñ  P  A  M  O  A  D  C  C  D  Ó  D  Í  O
M  I  R  S  R  A  U  A  A  R  C  B  A  Z  N  I  A  B  R  H  R
E  U  O  A  H  R  T  E  E  T  A  I  R  A  H  B  N  E  A  E  E
O  D  R  C  U  I  Ñ  G  J  E  D  G  B  E  A  Z  B  A  J  J  P
S  A  R  O  O  C  O  Á  A  A  M  J  O  L  H  U  E  R  T  A  O
P  E  P  A  R  U  D  A  R  R  E  C  C  H  T  E  S  Ó  L  C  R
P  T  T  F  V  E  N  T  A  N  A  Ó  V  E  S  T  Í  B  U  L  O
S  I  P  O  C  A  T  E  G  I  N  D  E  R  A  P  S  Í  L  L  E
```

AIR CONDITIONING

ATTIC/LOFT

AWNING

BALCONY

BASEMENT

BENCH

CABIN

CANOPY

CELLAR WINDOW

CLOAKROOM

CLOSET

COAT HANGER

COAT RACK

DOOR/GATE

DOORBELL

ENTRYWAY

FIREPLACE

FLOOR (STORY/LEVEL)

FLOOR (WALKABLE SURFACE)

FURNITURE

GARAGE

GARDEN

GARDEN (KITCHEN)

GARDEN WALL

GUTTER

HALLWAY

HANDRAIL

HEATING SYSTEM

HEDGE

HOME/HEARTH

HOUSE

HUT

IRON GRILLE (WINDOW)

LIGHTNING ROD

LOCK

MOLDING

PATIO

PLUMBING

RADIATOR

RETAINING WALL

ROOF

ROOM

SECURITY WALL

SHUTTERS

STAIRSTEP

STAIRWAY

STEP

SWIMMING POOL

TERRACE

VENETIAN BLINDS

WALK-IN CLOSET

WALL

WINDOW

Puzzle 21: It's A Living

Very few people like rearranging the furniture, but this puzzle shouldn't require too much heavy lifting on your part. The 22 English words below for things in a living room or den are arranged according to the number of letters in their Spanish translations; after you translate them, place the Spanish words in the grid. More than one word may fit in a particular space, but the overall solution is unique.

4 Letters

COUCH/SOFA
LIVING ROOM

5 Letters

BOOK
CLOCK
HEARTH
SEAT CUSHION

6 Letters

ARMCHAIR/LOUNGE CHAIR

7 Letters

DEN
DISPLAY CABINET
SPEAKER (STEREO)
STEREO\

8 Letters

ASHTRAY
CARPET
CURTAINS
FIREPLACE
TELEPHONE

9 Letters

DVD PLAYER (2 words)
TELEVISION SET

12 Letters

COFFEE TABLE (3 words)
ENCYCLOPEDIA
FAMILY ROOM (2 words)

14 Letters

VIDEO CASSETTE RECORDER

Puzzle 22: Mixed Signals

These electronic devices around the house are written in code — not the binary 0s and 1s in which computer signals are transmitted but a cryptogram. Using the English translations below and the first as an example, can you substitute the letters and effectively crack the code?

1. YDFUW = DISCO

2. EVYDW

3. VLJBLV

4. UVFBJB

5. BFUVLBE

6. BFJBEBW

7. VZJVKWUBF

8. VGYDSWLWF

9. VGEDUGZVE

10. UWTDVYWEV

11. TVNDLVYWE

12. PVLYV VLUAV

13. ZBUJWE YB UY

14. KDYBWUVHVEV

15. UWLJEWZ EBHWJW

16. UVHVEV YDNDJVZ

17. YDFUW UWHTVUJW

18. JBZBSWLW UBZGZVE

19. VZVEHV VLJDEEWPW

20. DLJBEUWHGLDUVYWE

21. EBTEWYGUJWE YB YKY

22. JEDJGEVYWEV YB TVTBZ

23. UWHTGJVYWEV TWEJVJDZ

24. FDFJBHV YB UDLB BL UVFV

25. UWHTGJVYWEV YB
    BFUEDJWEDW

26. JBZBKDFWE YB TVLJVZZV VLUAV

27. JBZBKDFWE YB TVLJVZZV TZVLV

ANTENNA	DESKTOP COMPUTER	PAGER
BROADBAND	DIGITAL CAMERA	PAPER SHREDDER
BURGLAR ALARM	DVD PLAYER	RADIO TRANSMITTER
CAMCORDER/VIDEO	FLAT-SCREEN TELEVISION	~~RECORD~~
CAMERA	HEADPHONES	REMOTE CONTROL
CASSETTE	HEADSET/EARPIECE	SCANNER
CD PLAYER	HOME THEATER SYSTEM	SPEAKERS
CELL/MOBILE PHONE	INTERCOM	STEREO
COMPACT DISC	LAPTOP/NOTEBOOK	WIDE-SCREEN TELEVISION
COPY MACHINE	COMPUTER	

Puzzle 23: Baby Talk

Unscramble the letter strings to form the Spanish words for baby-related items. The English equivalents for the scrambled Spanish words are listed after the puzzle.

1. NACU
2. NÉBEL
3. LÓMIV
4. TANAM
5. COALT
6. RETAIL
7. SÉMIOS
8. SPEÑALA
9. REOJONAS
10. BROMADICA
11. PLILARALMA

12. LISAL TALA
13. QUÍNDABAL
14. SOO ED CHULEPE
15. JACA ED SÚCIMA
16. TILISAL ED ESOPA
17. EGUJUTE ED PAROT
18. TECHIOCOC ED EBBÉ
19. PLASPEÑAROTA
20. SOLALITAT SHÚMEDA
21. CLIBATALO CREMEOD
22. CHIBATIÓNA ED SOL SNIÑO

BABY CARRIAGE	CRADLE	NURSERY
· BABY POWDER	CRIB	RATTLE
BABY WIPES	DIAPERS	ROCKING HORSE
BASSINET	DIAPER BAG	STROLLER
BED CANOPY	HIGH CHAIR	STUFFED TOY
BLANKET	MOBILE	TEDDY BEAR
BUNK BED	MUSIC BOX	
CHANGING TABLE	NIGHT LIGHT	

Puzzle 24: Table Settings

Translate the following words for items in a dining room, and then put them in their proper places in this fill-in grid. Words are listed in English and grouped according to the number of letters in their Spanish translations; more than word may fit in a particular space, but the overall solution is unique.

4 Letters

CUP
GOBLET
TABLE

5 Letters

CHAIR
HANDLE

6 Letters

BOWL
SOUP TUREEN
TABLECLOTH

7 Letters

DINING ROOM
FRUIT BOWL
GRAVY BOAT
JUG
SPOON
TABLETOP
TRAY

8 Letters

KNIFE
LADLE
PLACE SETTING
SIDEBOARD

9 Letters

CRUET
TEASPOON

10 Letters

BUTTER DISH
NAPKIN

13 Letters

COASTER/PLACEMAT
WALL UNIT (3 words)

14 Letters

CENTERPIECE (4 words)
DINNER SERVICE (3 words)

17 Letters

SERVING CART (3 words)

Puzzle 25: W.C. (Word Cross)

Knowing how to get directions to a bathroom and refer to the important items within it are critical topics for language-learners. (For obvious reasons, we think.) In this crossword, the clues are Spanish words for bathroom-related objects; fill their English equivalents in the grid.

Across

1 DUCHA
2 BAÑERA
6 ALFOMBRA DEL BAÑO (2 words)
9 BOTIQUÍN (2 words)
12 AZULEJO
13 CORTINA DE LA DUCHA (2 words)
14 PULVERIZADOR DE LA DUCHA
15 TOALLA

Down

1 JABONERA (2 words)
3 PAPEL HIGIÉNICO (2 words)
4 INODORO
5 LAVABO
7 TOALLERO (2 words)
8 BAÑO
10 CUARTO DE BAÑO
11 ESPONJA
13 BÁSCULA

Puzzle 26: Personal Matters

Many of us are a little disoriented first thing in the morning, but how quickly can you orient yourself to find the 44 Spanish words and phrases that pertain to hygiene and personal grooming? After you've found all the items on the list, you'll look your best and will be all set to face the day ahead.

```
V A L A T N E D O L I H C Á H O R Q U I L L A
A S E T N E I D S O L A R A P O L L I P E C O
A L L I C E D E R O D A E N I L E D P M C P D
S O M B R A D E O J O S M A É J J E Í E E O A
N L A Z E S R A T I E F A G N A I R O N P S N
S E N M C Z O V I Q E Q P N V N S D R J I T I
E P P U E U G A E U U S A E E A E A V U L I E
C L A E B R R D R N E L R A V N A L P A L Z P
A E J A L O C I Ó N D L A A T E G D R G O O T
D A A R R U Á R T U Q A A Í L B C Ñ Á U T L S
O R V I O E C R E A U D F G R L R O G E A A M
R A A C D R G A L L A R E B O T I Q U Í N C L
D P N S A Z N I P R I N I S Y S V U G N O A Á
E L G S S O R F O C R O T R O M O E Q L I P P
P E I N A R S E O N Ó B A J V D M V O A H A I
E G Ó Ú P M A H C M L O R Q F J O N L E M R Z
L U N A T E J A L L I U Q A M O I R N O Í A D
O Ñ C L A B Á S C U L A D E B A Ñ O A A P E E
C H U O L S C O S M É T I C O S E C A N Z L L
H A B E C R O D A N O I C I D N O C A D T P A
O N I E O M Á Q U I N A D E A F E I T A R E B
T E N A C I L L A P A R A E L P E L O H L L I
C E P I L L O P A R A E L P E L O B O S T O O
```

BANDAGE
BARRETTE
BATHROOM SCALE
BRUSH
COLOGNE
COMB (NOUN)
COMB (VERB)
CONDITIONER
COSMETICS
CREAM
CURLERS/ROLLERS
CURLING IRON

DENTAL FLOSS
DEODORANT
ELECTRIC SHAVER
EYELINER
EYE SHADOW
HAIRBRUSH
HAIRCLIP
HAIR DRYER
HAIR GEL
HAIRNET
HAIRPIECE
HAIRSPRAY

HAIRSTYLE
LIPSTICK
LOTION
MAKEUP (NOUN)
(TO APPLY)
  MAKEUP (VERB)
MASCARA
MEDICINE CABINET
MOUTHWASH
PLASTIC BANDAGE
POWDER
RAZOR

SHAMPOO
SHAVE (VERB)
SHAVING CREAM
SOAP
TALCUM POWDER
TOOTHBRUSH
TOOTHPASTE
TWEEZERS
WIG

Puzzle 27: Garden Party

Whether you grow plants, cultivate flowers, or harvest vegetables, consider yourself a master gardener if you complete this crossword about things found around the garden. The clues are in English; the words that you enter in the grid are their Spanish translations.

Across

3 GARDEN PATH

6 FLOWER POT

8 GREENHOUSE

10 SHOVEL

11 SPADE

13 INSECTICIDE

17 SPRINKLER

19 TROWEL

21 WEED

23 HEDGE

24 SHED

25 GARDEN

26 WATERING CAN

27 WHEELBARROW

Down

1 BASKET

2 GRASS

3 SEEDS

4 VEGETABLE GARDEN

5 GRASS SHEARS

7 LAWN MOWER

9 BUSH

12 PRUNING SHEARS (3 words)

14 FENCE

15 FERTILIZER

16 FLOWER BED

18 HOE

20 RAKE

22 HOSE

24 LAWN

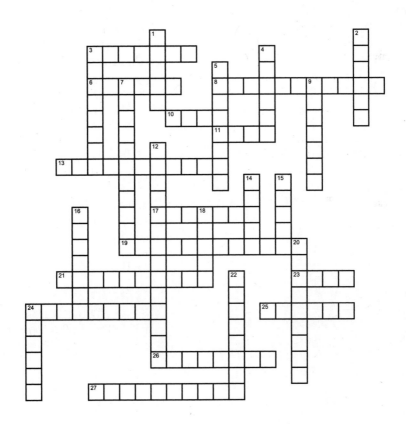

Puzzle 28: Party Time

In this puzzle, you get to fill in your social calendar with Spanish words and phrases associated with joyous occasions. The clues consist of their English equivalents, grouped by the lengths of the Spanish translations that fit into the grid. A word may fit in more than one position, but the overall solution is unique. Most importantly, enjoy yourself!

4 Letters

BABY
BOW (ON A GIFT)
WEDDING

5 Letters

BRIDE
CANDLES
GROOM
PHOTOGRAPHS
RIBBON

6 Letters

CAKE
GAMES
GIFT
MEAL
PARTY
RING

7 Letters

CARD
PROMOTION
REUNION

8 Letters

ENGAGEMENT
GUEST
SURPRISE

9 Letters

BLESSING

10 Letters

BIRTH
BIRTHDAY
HOLIDAY (2 words)
INVITATION
MARRIAGE
RETIREMENT

11 Letters

CELEBRATION
"CONGRATULATIONS!"
QUINCEAÑERA (Spanish party celebrating a girl's 15th birthday)

13 Letters

NEWLYWEDS (2 words)
WRAPPING PAPER (3 words)

Puzzle 29: What's Cooking?

Sleuth your way through the grid to find the Spanish words for 34 items you might find in a kitchen.

```
A L E S A C A C O R C H O S S E C H A
R N B E R Ó F C U C H A R A A Í R O L
E O I O Z O U A D C E C A H D É I F L
M L D C G Ñ T B A R R I T E N F A I O
I L F T O B S F E J N R I R O A N R R
C I A I D C E R F M O T C V O C A G A
N H R É Z T O E E M A C N I R E Q A R
E C Í G E D N N A P O É E D C D U B U
C U V R A C O G A T R L H O I O E I S
H C A T H P A D N E E E D R M L L N A
A G S U L R E S A N D A O E E L G E B
U O F A R R A G T E A N Ñ R D I I T A
T E C A A R A N I D G I E T O N R E T
O P D A T Z R E M O E C N E N I A I I
D O L É B O A V R R R O E R R L T E D
R C N A O L H E A E F C D M O O O Á O
É U Q R T R E R M M O N R O H M R L R
I A F R R O D A R E G I R F E R I N A
C A C E R O L A A T O C F R I G O O H
```

Puzzle 30: Fruit Stand

Decode the names of fruits from the coded entries that follow into their Spanish equivalents. You need to know the Spanish words for a dozen different fruits.

1. SMN YMOIMOMN = LAS MANZANAS (the apples)

2. SMN EUPMN

3. SMN OMPMOWMN

4. SZN SGYZOUN

5. SMN HZPZOWMN

6. SZN ESMHHOZN

7. SMN TUPUIMN

8. SMN TMSMQMIMN

9. SMN APMYQBUNMN

10. SMN APUNMN

11. SZN JBPMIOZN

12. SMN NMOJGMN

THE APPLES

THE BANANAS

THE CHERRIES

THE GRAPEFRUITS

THE LEMONS

THE ORANGES

THE PEACHES

THE PEARS

THE PUMPKINS

THE RASPBERRIES

THE STRAWBERRIES

THE WATERMELONS

Puzzle 31: Mixed Vegetables

The strings below contain the Spanish names of two vegetables with their letters in order, though not consecutively. Use your bean to form the two words.

Hint: The two vegetables in each string contain the same number of letters.

1. NAPABIOO		NABO	APIO
2. PAMAPÍAZ		_____	_____
3. PREÁBAPINONO		_____	_____
4. CELEBOCHUGLLA		_____	_____
5. COCOLILINAFLOBOR		_____	_____
6. GUIPISMIANENTETO		_____	_____
7. REBERENMOLAJECHANA		_____	_____
8. ZEANASPINAHORCASIA		_____	_____
9. ALESPÁCARRAGOCHOFA		_____	_____

ARTICHOKE	CORN	PEPPER
ASPARAGUS	CUCUMBER	POTATO
BEET	EGGPLANT	RADISH
CARROT	LETTUCE	RUTABAGA
CAULIFLOWER	ONION	SPINACH
~~CELERY~~	PEA	~~TURNIP~~

Puzzle 32: Ground Beef

The word fragments below consist of two, three, or four letters each, and when placed together form the names of various types or cuts of meat. The lengths of the word fragments along with their English translations are provided at right.

BIS	DERO	PA	TA
~~CA~~	EDE	POL	TEC
CARN	ILLA	PUE	TER
CHU	LE	RCO	VO
COR	LO	RES	
COST	NERO	~~RNE~~	

1. _____ CARNE _____ (2, 3)   MEAT

2. _____ (2, 2)   TURKEY

3. _____ (3, 2)   CHICKEN

4. _____ (3, 3)   PORK

5. _____ (3, 3)   STEAK

6. _____ (3, 4)   LAMB

7. _____ (3, 4)   VEAL

8. _____ (3, 2, 2)   CHOP

9. _____ (4, 4)   RIB

10. _____ (4, 3, 3) (3 words)   BEEF

Puzzle 33: Gone Fishing

Here's a puzzle with a hook to reel you in. Fourteen types of seafood appear in this aptly shaped body of water. Catch them all, and you'll not only have fish stories to tell but dinner for a week.

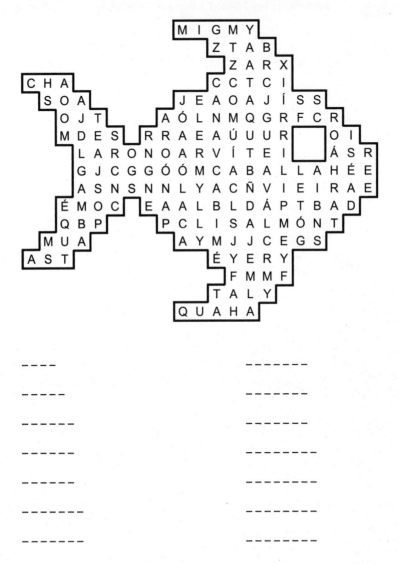

- - - -

- - - - -

- - - - - -

- - - - - -

- - - - - -

- - - - - - -

- - - - - -

- - - - - - -

- - - - - - -

- - - - - -

- - - - - - - -

- - - - - - -

- - - - - - -

- - - - - - -

Puzzle 34: Mixed Drinks

Rearrange the letter strings to spell the Spanish names for beverages. English translations appear below, except for the last seven, which are particularly popular in the Spanish-speaking world, and for which we provide brief descriptions rather than direct translations.

1. ÉT

2. FACÉ

3. AUGA

4. OVNI

5. OJUG

6. ADRIS

7. CHEEL

8. ÑACOC

9. MARTO

10. EBERB

11. LECTOC

12. DABBIE

13. SASEAGO

14. VEZCERA

15. ADILOMAN

16. PACHAÑAM

17. FERSCORE

18. UAGA LIMENAR

19. UAAG DELAMABOLTE

20. VACA (a Spanish variety of sparkling wine)

21. ANGRÍAS (a punch with red wine and fruit juice)

22. QUALITE (a Mexican agave-derived spirit)

23. CHATORAH (a non-dairy beverage usually consisting of nuts, grains, or legumes)

24. CHOMALICO (Kalimotxo, a Basque drink with wine and cola)

25. NOVI ED ZEJER (Sherry, a Spanish wine)

26. NOTTI ED ROVENA (a drink with wine and seltzer or some other soft drink)

BEER	JUICE
BOTTLED WATER	LEMONADE
BRANDY/COGNAC	MILK
CHAMPAGNE	MINERAL WATER
CIDER	SOFT DRINK
COCKTAIL	SODA/CARBONATED DRINK
COFFEE	TEA
DRINK (NOUN)	WATER
DRINK (VERB) (2 entries)	WINE

Puzzle 35: Just Desserts

Here's a puzzle that should satisfy your sweet tooth. Decode the following dessert words and phrases. English translations follow, except for the last seven, which are common in the Spanish-speaking world and for which we provide descriptions rather than translations.

1. ZAI FAIPOTI = LOS POSTRES (desserts)

2. TZ UZGC

3. ZG UOJPG

4. ZG PAOPG

5. TZ NJTIA

6. ZG QGCTZG

7. TZ FGIPTZ

8. TZ WTZGEA

9. ZAI EJZQTI

10. ZG VGZZTPG

11. TZ RGSGFGC

12. TZ IAOKTPT

13. ZAI EGPXZTI

14. ZG VTZGPXCG

15. TZ QGOGRTZA

16. TZ QWAQAZGPT

17. TZ EJZQT ET ZTQWT

18. TZ GOOAS QAC ZTQWT

19. ZGI BTRGI (sweet balls with egg yolks and powdered sugar)

20. TZ PJOOAC (Spanish halvah or brittle made with almonds and honey)

21. ZAI QWJOOAI (fried doughnut-like pastries)

22. TZ PTRKZTNJT (Puerto Rican coconut pudding)

23. ZAI FAZLAOACTI (crumbly cookies with powdered sugar)

24. ZG OAIQG ET OTBTI (sweet bread baked with trinkets, served on January 6)

25. ZGI QGZGLTOGI ET GSJQGO (sugar skulls baked for Día de los Muertos)

CAKE/PASTRY	~~DESSERTS~~
CANDY/SWEETS	FRUIT
CARAMEL SAUCE	GELATIN
CHEESE	HARD CANDY
CHOCOLATE	ICE CREAM
CINNAMON	MARZIPAN
COOKIE	PIE
CUSTARD	RICE PUDDING
DATES	SORBET

Chapter 5

Village and Countryside

● ●

Puzzle 36: Just What the Doctor Ordered

The sooner you've decoded this list of various doctors' remedies, the sooner you can feel better!

Hint: Two of the words that are most often used in Spanish in the plural form appear in the plural in this puzzle. You can probably spot them by their article.

1. ZB ZKOJKA = LA LOCIÓN

2. ZB CDTJOJAB

3. DZ SBZPBCK

4. ZB FBPRJZZB

5. ZB OBFPMZB

6. ZB FJZTKNB

7. ZBP BPFJNJABP

8. DZ FBNOYD

9. DZ MAWMDARK

10. DZ BARJTKRK

11. DZ JAYBZBTKN

12. DZ BARJSJKRJOK

13. DZ BARJYJPRBCJAJOK

14. ZKP CDTJOBCDARKP

15. ZB FBPRJZZB FBNB ZB RKP

16. DZ TDPOKAWDPRJKABARD

ANTIBIOTIC

ANTIDOTE

ANTIHISTAMINE

ASPIRIN

CAPSULE

COUGH DROP/LOZENGE

DECONGESTANT

INHALER

~~LOTION~~

MEDICATION

MEDICINE

OINTMENT

PATCH

PILL

SALVE

TABLET

Puzzle 37: What's in Store

Given the Spanish words for types of stores in the crossword clues, fill in the English word in the crossword grid for the items sold there.

Hint: You'll notice that *-ería* is a common suffix to many of these clues. It means "store," so knowing the root word to which it's added should be helpful to you.

Across

3 JOYERÍA

4 LIBRERÍA

5 ROPERÍA

8 DULCERÍA

9 FRUTERÍA

10 BODEGA/SUPERMERCADO

15 CARNICERÍA

16 JUGUETERÍA

17 TIENDA DE RECUERDOS

18 FERRETERÍA

20 PAPELERÍA

21 PANADERÍA

Down

1 VERDULERÍA

2 BOTICA/FARMACIA

6 ZAPATERÍA

7 TIENDA DE ANTIGÜEDADES

9 MUEBLERÍA

11 CAFETERÍA

12 AGENCIA DE SEGUROS

13 PASTELERÍA

14 SOMBRERERÍA

19 GALERÍA DE ARTE

Puzzle 38: Lost in the Mail

Neither snow nor rain nor dark nor gloom of night should keep you from making your appointed rounds. Complete your delivery route by finding the Spanish translations for the English words and phrases pertaining to the post office. Some English words have two Spanish equivalents that appear in the grid separately; these are tagged "(2 entries)." For verbs, the infinitive form is hidden.

```
P M A N D A R E R V A P A R T A D O
M A S O L S O L L E S A T A M L E R
X T Q U A E E A E G R E A A G I R O
G A G U O L N T T S R J L N C T A C
P S D C E A Á N R F A R N L L U E R
C E C A R T A E O C L A Ó Á A F Q F
Ó L C É É S E I P S E C I L S R O R
D L H I A O E D E A R I C O I E I A
I A L D O P O N D L C F C E F M R N
G R E S E A C E O L A I E T I A A Q
O C D E R T O P C I R S R N C L T U
P I R L R E R E N P T A I E A Á A E
O N O L O J R D A M E L D T D R N O
S T C O C R E Í R A R C Q I O A I B
T A Ó R A A O C F T O U Á M R I T U
A O L E S T E H A S O B R E A V S Z
L É L A I C E P S E A G E R T N E Ó
R Q O Í V N E E D S O T S A G E D N
```

ADDRESS

ADDRESSEE

AIR MAIL (2 words)

BOX

CANCEL/POSTMARK (VERB)

CLERK (fem.)

ENVELOPE

FREE SHIPPING (3 words)

LETTER

LETTER CARRIER (masc.)

LICK (VERB)

MAILBOX

MONEY ORDER

PACKAGE

POST OFFICE

POST OFFICE BOX

POSTAGE

POSTAGE AND HANDLING
 (3 words)

POSTCARD (2 words)

POSTMARK (noun)

SEAL (VERB)

SEND (2 entries)

SENDER

SORT (VERB)

SORTING MACHINE

SPECIAL DELIVERY (2 words)

STAMP (2 entries)

STRING

TAPE

ZIP/POSTAL CODE (2 words)

Puzzle 39: At Your Service

The 21 words below refer to buildings and various services you might find in your city or town. Translate them from English to their Spanish equivalents and enter them into the grid. More than one word may fill in any particular space, but the overall solution is unique. Three of the words are exact cognates.

Hint: The words are grouped by the number of letters in their Spanish translation. Don't include articles in the translations.

3 Letters
BAR

4 Letters
MOVIE THEATER

5 Letters
BANK
COURTHOUSE
HOTEL
MUSEUM

7 Letters
SCHOOL

8 Letters
BARBER SHOP
HOSPITAL

9 Letters
FUNERAL HOME
TECHNICAL SCHOOL

10 Letters
DRY CLEANERS
LAUNDRY
LIBRARY

11 Letters
RESTAURANT

12 Letters
CITY HALL

14 Letters
BEAUTY SALON (3 words)
GARAGE (MECHANIC SHOP) (2 words)

15 Letters
TRAVEL AGENCY (3 words)

16 Letters
FIREHOUSE (3 words)

18 Letters
POLICE STATION (3 words)

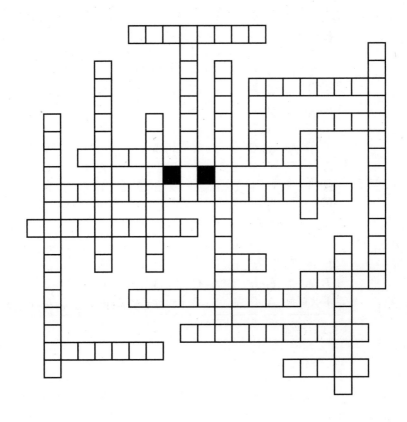

Puzzle 40: Town Meeting

In the grid below, look for 37 things that you might see in a city. Note that one word has two different meanings that fit the category, and so you're looking for 36 words.

```
Z I O A M B U L A N C I A S P E N A T
L X C R F H N Ó I C C E S R E T N I I
O A C C O R R E D E P O L A C Í A B E
I T E O I F B O C A C A L L E C R A N
D P N C C S Á R A U T O B Ú S R R N D
N E T A H H S M F L L A Ñ E S A I C A
E D R N B J E A E C O I R R A B L O G
C I O C R I R D C S C R U C E Z O A B
N S C H C O C H E D E B O M B E R O S
I T O A L E B I N P L A Z A P A T R E
E R M L C U L U C Ó O R E Ó J V E R N
D I E T S E I I L L I L A E A E M E D
A T R E I D R E F E E M I R E N Á T E
C O C H E B S A A S V T A C M I R N R
O E I A H T S M F R E A A C Í D B E O
B P A R A D A O R Á M D R Y N A O U G
E X L D E R B M U D E H C U M M L P Í
T A I E S T A C I Ó N D E T R E N E S
I O R A P A S O D E P E A T O N E S A
```

Puzzle 41: Civic Center

It's your civic duty to find the 50 Spanish words that relate to local, state, and national government and politics. The words include governmental titles and political organizations and affiliations. Many of the Spanish words in the grid are similar to their English equivalents.

```
L C H Ó F Z B O O O C I T Á M O L P I D Á L E
A A E T N E D I S E R P E C I V R O D A N E S
R R R E P U B L I C A N O U N T I T U L A R D
E L G C A J P E L L I G A O Y E M R O M D I I
D A A O F I C I N A E Ñ E G S A O D A D N O C
E N O L Z C O L O N I A E N I E A L Í A E A T
F O D E A R E F T O F S G C C O R O L N I E A
X I I G A N R U O L T T A I F I R G A C M L D
C C P I O L E R V A A R E Ó L E A E N E N B O
O A L O M B E G D C C O D A N E S B L O E M R
N N O E U P E O O O O I L O T I P A C O C A A
S S M L N M U R M X N H C O L A R F D A T S Y
E E A E I U T E N P A R L A M E N T O T E A U
R C C C C E D A S A T X E H B I V O T A R E N
V R I T I R R A H T D N Ó I C C E L E R E L T
A E A O P Á N I C U O O L O B E O Ñ O C A E A
D T N R A D A D U I C V R E O O N O T Ó D G M
O A M A L T A L C A L D E D Y I G S I M O I I
R R A L T R I B U N A L S U P R E M O E V R E
Y I C A D D E P A R T A M E N T O D Q D E M N
E O R T S I N I M R E M I R P E T I C I Ó N T
D A N O R G E N Ó I C U T I T S N O C T C A O
R E P R E S E N T A N T E E T N E D I S E R P
```

Puzzle 42: Bank on It

If money talks, then we hope you've heard all the Spanish words related to banking and finance that this crossword features. Clues are provided in English; insert their Spanish translations in the grid.

Across

1 INTEREST

5 CHANGE (VERB)

6 CHECK

7 CASH (2 words)

9 TELLER WINDOW

10 PAYMENT

11 RETURN

12 CHARGE (VERB)

14 PAY

17 BANK

18 MONEY

19 LEND

20 FEE

21 AUTOMATIC TELLER MACHINE (2 words)

23 CHANGE

24 CHECKING ACCOUNT (2 words)

Down

2 CREDIT CARD (3 words)

3 BANKER

4 MONEY ORDER (2 words)

5 SAVINGS ACCOUNT (3 words)

8 ENDORSE

13 SAVE

14 LOAN

15 BILL (PAPER MONEY/ BANK NOTE)

16 EARN

22 CHANGE/EXCHANGE

Puzzle 43: Out to Lunch

The items on this menu are words and phrases related to dining out. Can you set them right given the scrambled strings of letters and the list of English translations that follow?

1. LAS = SAL
2. FACÉ
3. POCA
4. SAME
5. EMÚN
6. POSA
7. SOVA
8. RABRA
9. TARCA
10. DUCOR
11. LOPTA
12. LISLA
13. CEITEA
14. A NOPUT
15. DABIBE
16. DAMICO
17. TENUCA
18. SAREEM
19. MORESE
20. POSTER
21. PICÁNTA
22. CHURACA
23. PIAPRON

24. CORPIÓN
25. ASERVER
26. DORENTE
27. REAVING
28. A AL RATAC
29. CORECION
30. COTRUIBE
31. HUCILLOC
32. DALANEAS
33. STRÉNEME
34. PANTIEMI
35. VICEROIS
36. TERÍAFECA
37. CARCHUATI
38. COOP ECHOH
39. NEBI DIOCCO
40. TRAVELLIES
41. NUBE VORCHOPE
42. ALTOP CLAPIPRIN
43. PAÑAMACOTIMENO
44. DUANTEYA ED RORACEMA
45. PLIEDASADICE ED AL ASCA

A LA CARTE

APPETIZER

BEVERAGE/DRINK

BILL/CHECK

BUSBOY

CAFÉ

CAFETERIA

CHAIR

CHEF, COOK

COUNTER

DESSERT

"ENJOY YOUR MEAL!"

ENTRÉE

FORK

GLASS

GOBLET

HEADWAITER

HOUSE SPECIAL

KNIFE

MEAL

MEDIUM

MENU (OFFERINGS)

MENU (PRINTED)

NAPKIN

OIL

PEPPER (SEASONING)

PLATE

PORTION

RARE (NOT WELL-DONE)

RAW

RESERVATION

SALAD

~~SALT~~

SERVICE/SERVICE
    CHARGE

SIDE DISH

SOUP

SPOON

TABLE

TABLE SETTING

TEASPOON

TIP

VINEGAR

WAITER

WAITRESS

WELL-DONE

Puzzle 44: To Your Health

Here's hoping you don't have to visit a doctor's office or hospital for more than a routine checkup. However, accidents and emergencies happen, either at home or while traveling, and so the vocabulary words hidden in this puzzle are worth knowing. Find the Spanish words in the grid given their English translations on the next page.

```
E S C A L O F R Í O S V S A O N A F Ó R I U Q
P U S A I C N E G R U E D A L A S P O C C C J
O A R F I A Y R M A I C N A L U B M A A U I C
C A N T I H I S T A M Í N I C O R Q M P B R E
N H V F N P T J A É P A I J V E O A N E P U A
Í D S V E E L L D B M R E S F R I A D O H J C
S A T O G O U I G O H N R N R P Í L D O R A C
J C N A C S C A T A Q U E A L C O R A Z Ó N I
C F C I P O P N D P A S T I L L A Q H H O O D
O F Ó Á C L Í N I C A A E G A I R T F L A H E
N N C O N S T I P A C I Ó N J E B I E Q G L N
S I N Y E C C I Ó N D E M E R G E N C I A G T
U O C I R U G Í A M H D E P C B O V E N D A E
L X T O N E G Í X O O O A N R R É G I M E N R
T A M P O L L A S L Z C C E F E J S F M A L M
O J Q Y Z B E P O S I L L A D E R U E D A S Ó
R T E C G T I R R E F Q A S P I R I N A S E M
I S R F T T O T N E I M I C A N V M A I C T E
O P V A A A N T I B I Ó T I C O U U E B J R T
I A T L P Z E N F E R M E D A D I Z Z R X E R
R A D I O G R A F Í A P U L M O N Í A G O U O
I N H A L A D O R B M E D I C I N A Q P V M G
E V O P E R A C I Ó N Z B O E M B A R A Z O R
```

ACCIDENT	HOSPITAL
ACHE	I.C.U. (abbreviation)
AMBULANCE	ILL/SICK
ANTIBIOTIC	ILLNESS/SICKNESS
ANTIHISTAMINE	INHALER
ASPIRIN	INJECTION
BANDAGE	LOTION
BED	MEDICINE
BIRTH	MEDICINE DROPS
BLISTER	NASAL CONGESTION
CAPSULE	NURSE
CHEST COLD	OPERATING ROOM
CHILLS	OPERATION
CLINIC	OXYGEN
COUGH	PATIENT
CURE	PILL
DEATH	PLASTER CAST
DIET (PLAN)	PNEUMONIA
DIET (SELECTION)	PREGNANCY
DOCTOR	SURGEON
DOCTOR'S OFFICE	SURGERY
EMERGENCY	SYMPTOM
EMERGENCY ROOM	TABLET
FAINTING SPELL	THERMOMETER
FEVER	TRIAGE
FLU	WHEELCHAIR
HEAD COLD	X-RAY
HEART ATTACK	

Puzzle 45: Working It Out

Translate these English words for people and things you might find in an office environment, and place their Spanish equivalents in the grid. Fill in all 24 words in their correct position and you'll definitely be under consideration for a raise!

Hint: The words are grouped by the number of letters in their Spanish translation. Don't include articles in the translations.

3 Letters
NETWORK

4 Letters
BOSS (masc.)
ERASER

5 Letters
CHAIR
CLOCK
(COMPUTER) MOUSE
PAPER
PENCIL
TAPE

6 Letters
JOB

7 Letters
BRIEFCASE
LAMP
MANAGER (masc./fem.)
MONITOR
OFFICE

8 Letters
SCREEN
TELEPHONE

9 Letters
BOSS (fem.)
PEN
PRINTER

10 Letters
DESK

11 Letters
COMPUTER
STAPLER

17 Letters
E-MAIL (2 words)

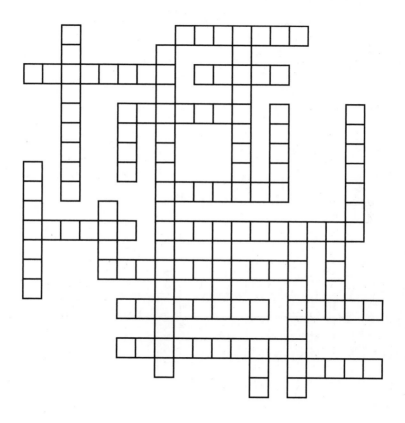

Puzzle 46: Subject Matter

Translate the school subjects below from English and enter their Spanish equivalents in the crossword grid. Complete the puzzle to be a straight-A student!

Across

1 MUSIC

5 HISTORY

9 MATHEMATICS

10 LAW

Down

2 ART

3 ARCHITECTURE

4 CHEMISTRY

6 ENGINEERING

7 PHYSICS

8 JOURNALISM

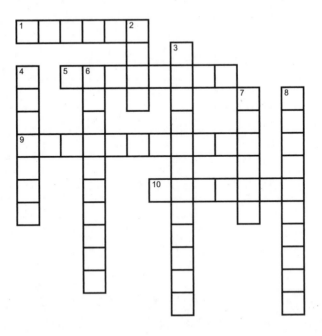

Puzzle 47: A Touch of Class

The first day of school can be a little disorienting, but you move to the head of the class when you find the Spanish equivalents of all 30 English words associated with a classroom.

```
N E M A X E A L A R T S E A M
A E O T J M I L E C C I Ó N E
A P N R O B N E M U S E R R Z
P C R G R A L U M N O E T C G
U O E O A R R A Z I P I T X O
N N D A Y A B E U R P E Z R R
T O A Í N I X Q C U T R T I A
E C U F V D Q J P N E S A R S
S I C A L U M N A D E L A L A
C M R R Y T A T N A I H E S P
R I A G R S S E M H C T C L E
I E S O X E R X C U R E Z E R
B N N N M P V O C A T O N P J
I T E O A H M S C T A R E A U
R O P M D H E N S E Ñ A R P O
```

Nouns

BACKPACK	NOTES
BLACKBOARD	PAPER
BOOK	POSTER
DESK	QUIZ
ERASER	SHELF
EXAM	STUDENT (fem.)
GRADE	STUDENT (masc.)
HOMEWORK	SUMMARY
KNOWLEDGE	TEACHER (fem.)
LESSON	TEACHER (masc.)
NOTEBOOK	TERM PAPER

Verbs (inf.)

LEARN
LISTEN
READ
REVIEW
STUDY
TEACH
THINK
WRITE

Puzzle 48: What's My Line?

Your job? To find the 41 occupations in this secret word list puzzle.

Hint: Some terms are unique to a particular gender (such as *actor* and *actriz*), others are gender-neutral (such as *artista*), and the remainder are masculine but take the feminine form when their suffix changes; these occupations are divided roughly equally between masculine and feminine.

```
B O M B E R A G R I C U L T O R M A R
O C I N C É T P A A T S I D O I R E P
O R E M O L P T O C L I Ñ A B L A A O
I J E P Y N Í R A L I A B T L A T R D
N D R S O E C A R P I N T E R A E O E
E E O A E E S L O I O C Á D U B L S N
M P D S Z M T R T U H R Í C R Í T T T
S E A T A R E A C Q C A T A E A A R I
E N T R Ñ F R L A J R G B S P M A O S
C D N E O Z L U D E A M R R E R J D T
R I O H I A T N N D L R E A O A V E A
E E C P A O R I A M S S D T Í E M D T
T N E O R E C E P C I O N I S T A N S
A T R S A O A J T D I I L H N G Á E I
R A R Z C Ñ B P E R P D P D O E Q V T
I S E Q E E T N E G A I É B A L R U R
A U N U R P T Z I R T C A M H D U A A
J Q D E N E Ó N E N F E R M E R O Z E
C O M E R C I A N T E T N E T S I S A
```

Puzzle 49: Computer Language

Computers are such a central part of our lives (this puzzle was written with the help of one!) that their unique terminology is very important to store in *your* memory. Thirty-seven Spanish computer-related terms appear in this grid. Can you find them given the list of their English translations?

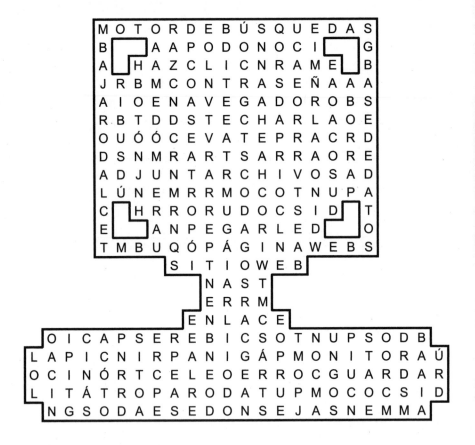

```
M O T O R D E B Ú S Q U E D A S
B       A A P O D O N O C I     G
A   H A Z C L I C N R A M E   B
J R B M C O N T R A S E Ñ A A A
A I O E N A V E G A D O R O B S
R B T D D S T E C H A R L A O E
O U Ó Ó C E V A T E P R A C R D
D S N M R A R T S A R R A O R E
A D J U N T A R C H I V O S A D
L Ú N E M R R M O C O T N U P A
C   H R R O R U D O C S I D   T
E     A N P E G A R L E D     O
T M B U Q Ó P Á G I N A W E B S
        S I T I O W E B
        N A S T
        E R R M
        E N L A C E
O I C A P S E R E B I C S O T N U P S O D B
L A P I C N I R P A N I G Á P M O N I T O R A Ú
O C I N Ó R T C E L E O E R R O C G U A R D A R
L I T Á T R O P A R O D A T U P M O C O C S I D
N G S O D A E S E D O N S E J A S N E M M A
```

AT SIGN (@)

ATTACH (AS A FILE)

BOOKMARK (A WEB SITE)

BROWSER

BUTTON

CHAT (NOUN)

CLICK (COMMAND, AS A LINK)
   (2 words)

COLON (IN A WEB ADDRESS)
   (2 words)

CYBERSPACE

DATABASE (3 words)

DISK

DOT COM (2 words)

DOWNLOAD (VERB)

DRAG

E-MAIL (VERB) (2 words)

FILES

FOLDER

HARD DRIVE (2 words)

HOME PAGE (2 words)

ICON

INTERNET/NETWORK

KEYBOARD

LAPTOP COMPUTER (2 words)

LINK (NOUN)

MENU

MODEM

MONITOR

MOUSE

PASSWORD

SCREEN NAME

SEARCH ENGINE (3 words)

SLASH

SPAM (3 words)

SURF (VERB)

UPLOAD (VERB)

WEB PAGE (2 words)

WEB SITE (2 words)

Puzzle 50: Good Sports

The English translations of 25 Spanish sports can be found in this crossword. Complete the grid and you'll enter the winner's circle of puzzle solvers.

Across

5 EL HOCKEY

6 EL SURF

8 EL ESQUÍ EN TABLA

10 EL CULTURISMO

12 EL VOLEIBOL

14 EL BALONCESTO

16 EL ESQUÍ

18 LA NATACIÓN

19 LA CORRIDA DE TOROS

21 EL BOXEO

22 EL BALONMANO

23 EL ATLETISMO

24 EL FÚTBOL

Down

1 LA LUCHA LIBRE

2 EL CICLISMO

3 EL LEVANTAMIENTO DE PESAS

4 EL FÚTBOL AMERICANO

7 EL RACQUETBOL

9 LA ESGRIMA

11 EL PATINAJE SOBRE HIELO
    (2 words)

13 LOS SALTOS

15 EL BÉISBOL

17 EL GOLF

18 EL BÉISBOL DE PELOTA BLANDA

20 EL TENIS

Puzzle 51: Games People Play

Given the English translations for various games and gaming equipment below, can you enter their Spanish equivalents in the grid? The words are grouped according to the length of their Spanish translations.

4 Letters
JACKS

5 Letters
CHECKERS
DICE

6 Letters
BALL
DARTS
DOMINOES
JUMP ROPE
(PLAYING) CARDS
POOL/BILLIARDS

7 Letters
CHESS
GAME (MATCH/COMPETITION)
GAME BOARD
HOPSCOTCH
HOUSE
MARBLES
RACE

8 Letters
PING-PONG

9 Letters
HIDE AND SEEK

10 Letters
CROSSWORD PUZZLE

11 Letters
BOARD GAME (3 words)

12 Letters
BATTLESHIP (2 words)
PUZZLE

15 Letters
TAG (4 words)

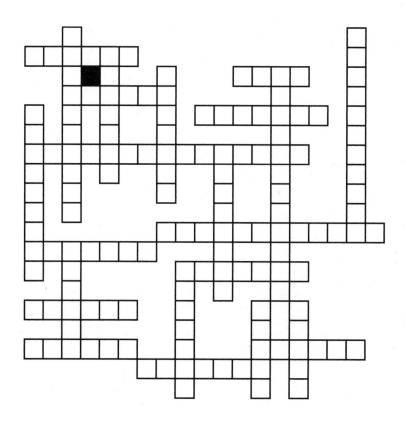

Puzzle 52: Channel Surfing

Given the Spanish terms for types of television shows, can you find their English translations in the word search grid?

```
T S A C S W E N V X L T R L N T O A S I
G H A C O U R A M A R D O L E M A W H L
C V Y O I S Y E P Y R E T S Y M A P I H
X A M A R D E M I R C V E W P N U V E B
C Q T N E M N I A T R E T N E O E U D D
V O A O C E K G N I M M A R G O R P X O
T A L K S H O W Y E E M O C T I S T Z W
T A R O R T B R P T A B N R D Y U F S O
P W Q I R C E O T T R L A C G G A L A H
E M S W E A M E H O W V A O I N S P R S
Q M E S L T N H A O E N L I T N R T E S
U M F I J O Y D H L C O O A R O P S P N
I P T Y M D C S O D H W S O G E T E O E
Z Y X R C A S G H T O Y O R T X S T P R
S S E R S D U Y N O E K A H L R P N A D
H S W T R E C A Q U W M B U S N A O O L
O L I A Q N O I T C I F E C N E I C S I
W N W N A T U R E P R O G R A M M C S H
G A D O C U M E N T A R Y M Q M C A O C
O R M M U E T I H W D N A K C A L B G M
```

ANTOLOGÍA

BLANCO Y NEGRO
(3 words)

CIENCIA FICCIÓN (2 words)

COLOR

COMEDIA SITUACIONAL

CONCURSO

DIBUJO ANIMADO

DOCUMENTAL

DOCUMENTAL DE VIAJE

DOCUMENTAL SOBRE LA
NATURALEZA (2 words)

DRAMÓN

ENTRETENIMIENTO

EN VIVO

ESPECTÁCULO DE
PREMIOS (2 words)

ESPECTÁCULO DE
VARIEDADES (2 words)

FANTASÍA

GRABADO

HISTORIA POLICÍACA
(2 words)

MISTERIO

NOTICIERO

PROGRAMA

PROGRAMA DE
CONCURSO (2 words)

PROGRAMA DE
DEPORTES

PROGRAMA DE
ENTREVISTAS (2 words)

PROGRAMA DE JUEGO
(2 words)

PROGRAMA PARA NIÑOS
(2 words)

PROGRAMACIÓN

SERIAL

SERMÓN

TELEDIFUSIÓN

TELENOVELA (2 words)

TELEREALIDAD

Puzzle 53: Look It Up

You find these words and phrases related to the library by wandering the stacks in this grid, across, down, and diagonally.

```
T P E D I R P R E S T A D O U F S M É N O Z E
A T I B O T N E I M I C N E V E D A H C E F S
R É N Ó I C A V O N E R L A D E V O L V E R T
J R S A L A D E L E C T U R A A S O I T R Ó A
E A G O B B I B L I O T E C A I N R E J A I N
T N F I C H E R O N E O C H R P Ú B L I C O T
A E A R O D A T U P M O C I A O M I E A R U E
D D H O N A N P A O D R A V G C E L T D I Q R
I R C D P U Ú U Í C E O O A E N R I N N C E Í
C O E A R N M B R I N R I R R A O L A Ó V S A
C C F H E Ó E L E L O A R P T Y A H T I R U D
I I I C S P R I T B P L A R N R N O S C O M E
O D D E T M O C N Ú I P U A E Ó I T E I T A F
N Ó O F A A D A A P J M S C I F A D I D C S I
A I C V R T E R T R O E U C D R E T E E E I C
R R U O D O C L S E C J C O C A R R L P L L H
I E M L O L A N E C H E R A H C E F E U R E E
O P E U N L T C L A S I F I C A C I Ó N M N R
S A N M A E Á R R H T O N D A S M I Z A C C O
E C T E N S L I B R O D E C O N S U L T A I S
R H O N T S O R B I L E D O T I S Ó P E D O A
I O R N E R G L L O I R A C E T O I L B I B C
E N C I C L O P E D I A S U S C R I P C I Ó N
```

ATLAS

BOOK

BOOK DEPOSIT (3 words)

BORROW (2 words)

CALL NUMBER (3 words)

CARD

CARD CATALOG (3 words)

CLASSIFICATION

COMPUTER

COPY (OF A BOOK)

DATE (NOUN)

DATE-STAMP (NOUN)

DATE-STAMP (VERB)

DICTIONARY

DOCUMENT

DONOR

DUE DATE (3 words)

EDITION

ENCYCLOPEDIA

FEE

FILE (VERB)

FINE

ISSUE (NOUN)

ISSUE (VERB) (2 words)

LEND

LIBRARIAN

LIBRARY

LIBRARY CATALOG

LIBRARY PATRON

LIBRARY STACKS

MAGAZINE

NEWSPAPER

PHOTOCOPY

PUBLIC

PUBLISH

READER

READING ROOM (3 words)

REFERENCE

REFERENCE BOOK (3 words)

RENEWAL

REQUEST (VERB)

RETURN (VERB)

RUBBER STAMP (2 words)

SECTION

SERIES

SHELF

SILENCE

SORT (VERB)

SUBSCRIPTION

TAKE OUT (VERB)

TURN IN (VERB)

VOLUME

Puzzle 54: Shuffling the Deck

Unscramble the Spanish word for each card game below. The last four are card games popular in Spanish-speaking countries; we don't provide English translations for those games. After you successfully deal out all the correct names, cash in your chips as a winner at anagramming.

1. KERPÓ

2. YMUMR

3. GEBIRD

4. SCATANA

5. HOCO COLO

6. ARITOLISO

7. NUEVITINO

8. SUM

9. ZOOP

10. NÓCHINCH

11. LANENTCOINT

BLACKJACK

BRIDGE

CANASTA

CRAZY EIGHTS

POKER

RUMMY

SOLITAIRE

Chapter 6
The Natural World

Puzzle 55: Precious Cargo

The Spanish words for gems and precious stones in this puzzle are encoded as cryptograms. Using the first as an example to help you get started, can you logically decode the rest of the list?

Hint: The first twelve entries in this puzzle are official birthstones (traditional and modern) for each of the twelve months in their calendar order. The other five entries are the Spanish words for aquamarine, beryl, carnelian, ivory, and lapis lazuli.

1. LA UIZJZRL

    EL GRANATE   GARNET

2. AZ ZDZRCMRZ

3. AZ MZJUSCJZICZ

4. LA YCZDZJRL

5. AZ LMDLIZAYZ

6. AZ QLIAZ

7. LA ISNC

_____   _____

8. LA QLICYFRF

_____   _____

9. LA PZKCIF

_____   _____

10. LA FQZAF

_____   _____

11. LA RFQZVCF

_____   _____

12. LA VCIVFJ

_____   _____

13. LA AZQCMAZPSAC

_____   _____

14. AZ VFIJZACJZ

_____   _____

15. LA NLICAF

_____   _____

16. LA DZIKCA

_____   _____

17. AZ ZUSZDZICJZ

_____   _____

Puzzle 56: Face Time

Perform plastic surgery by rearranging the Spanish words for the face and its features. (Their English equivalents appear below the puzzle to help you out.) When you correctly unscramble the words, the letters above the numbered spaces spell out, in order, another Spanish word for where these body parts can be found.

1. ARCA   C A R A   FACE
             1

2. AÑAPESTS   _ _ _ _ _ _ _ _

3. GULENA   _ _ _ _ _ _
             2

4. TIDENSE   _ _ _ _ _ _ _

5. JESCA   _ _ _ _ _

6. SIBALO   _ _ _ _ _ _
             3

7. FENTER   _ _ _ _ _ _

8. USTIC   _ _ _ _ _

9. ROJESA   _ _ _ _ _ _
             4

10. CABO   _ _ _ _

11. RINZA   _ _ _ _ _
             5

12. SOJO   _ _ _ _

13. SODÍO   _ _ _ _ _

14. CEBOLLA   _ _ _ _ _ _ _
             6

COMPLEXION	EYELASHES	MOUTH
EARS (INNER)	~~FACE~~	NOSE
EARS (OUTER)	FOREHEAD	TEETH
EYES	HAIR	TONGUE
EYEBROWS	LIPS	

Puzzle 57: Body of Knowledge

Add the one or two letters provided to each English word, and then rearrange the new string to spell the Spanish word for a part of the human body. (English words for these body parts are listed after the puzzle.)

Hint: Accent marks may appear in the Spanish word but not necessarily in the corresponding letters of the English word at left. Number 25 is an example of this.

1. JO + O = OJO

2. PI + E

3. COO + D

4. ARC + A

5. ODD + E

6. MOA + N

7. CAB + O

8. ACE + J

9. LIP + E

10. POL + E

11. SOUL + M

12. RAIN + Z

13. BAIL + O

14. LINE + G

15. BOAR + Z

16. HOPE + C

17. RANGE + S

18. TINED + E

19. CEDAR + A

20. ANGEL + U

21. RIPEN + A

22. CELLO + U

23. DOLLAR + I

24. ORATES + R

25. CORONA + Z

26. PLEADS + A

27. OIL + DUN + L

28. AISLE + PIN + L

29. PALLOR + RANT + I

30. JAR + EO

31. LAX + AI

32. PLUM + ÓN

33. CAME + ÑU

34. FEET + RN

35. PASTE + AÑ

36. CORER + BE

37. ANTIC + UR

38. LILACS + TO

39. RAGTAG + AN

40. OMEGAS + TÓ

41. IDLE DEED + PO = (3 words)

ARM	FINGER	NECK
ARMPIT	FOOT	NOSE
BACK	FOREHEAD	RIB
BLOOD	GROIN	SHIN
BRAIN	HAIR	SKIN
BUTTOCKS	HAND	STOMACH
CALF	HEART	THIGH
CHEST	HIP	THROAT
EAR	KNEE	TOE
ELBOW	KNUCKLE	TONGUE
EYE	LEG	TOOTH
EYEBROW	LIP	WAIST
EYELASH	LUNG	WRIST
FACE	MOUTH	

Puzzle 58: Bird Sanctuary

You certainly won't be a birdbrain if you find all the words here. Don't duck the chance to crow about your eagle-eyed solving prowess. Translate these names of birds from English to Spanish and locate them in the grid below.

```
O T A P S P Á G U I L A A
A V V L B U I T R E G F Z
Ñ H E D C G A N S O A A O
E F S P I A T A G J L I R
Ü Z T E R T T A Í Ü L S N
G B R R Q N R R P X I Á U
I O U I Ó Z B O A U N N E
C I Z C A I R A V Z A N O
B R L O L O M E O J S G V
U A G O L O N D R I N A R
H N C V L A H Z C C N L E
O A G A V I O T A L B L U
A C P O L L U E L O D O C
```

CANARY	GANNET	OWL	STORK
CHICK	GOOSE	PARAKEET	SWALLOW
CROW	HAWK	PARROT	SWAN
DOVE	HEN	PENGUIN	TURKEY
DUCK	HERON	PHEASANT	VULTURE
EAGLE	HUMMINGBIRD	ROOSTER	
FALCON	OSTRICH	SEAGULL	

Puzzle 59: Forecast of Characters

Sixteen weather-related words appear on this map of North America. They show up on the map in roughly the areas where they're likely to occur. Clear up the mess by finding all 16 and there'll be nothing but blue skies.

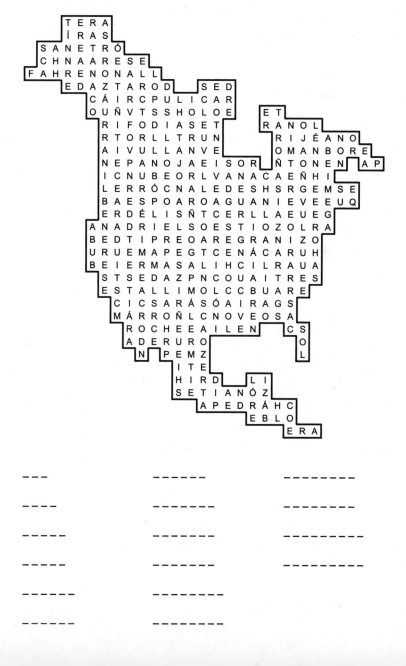


```
        T E R A
        Í R A S
    S A N E T R Ó
    C H N A A R E S E
  F A H R E N O N A L L
    E D A Z T A R O D     S E D
      C Á I R C P U L I C A R
      O U Ñ V T S S H O L O E     E T
      R I F O D I A S E T       R A N O L
      R T O R L L T R U N       R I J É A N O
      A I V U L L A N V E       O M A N B O R E
      N E P A N O J A E I S O R   Ñ T O N E N   A P
      I C N U B E O R L V A N A C A E Ñ H I
      L E R R Ó C N A L E D E S H S R G E M S E
      B A E S P O A R O A G U A N I E V E E U Q
      E R D É L I S Ñ T C E R L L A E U E G
    A N A D R I E L S O E S T I O Z O L R A
    B E D T I P R E O A R E G R A N I Z O
    U R U E M A P E G T C E N Á C A R U H
    B E I E R M A S A L I H C I L R A U A
      S T S E D A Z P N C O U A I T R E S
      E S T A L L I M O L C C B U A R E
        C I C S A R Á S Ó A I R A G S
        M Á R R O Ñ L C N O V E O S A
        R O C H E E A I L E N   C S
        A D E R U R O       O L
          N   P E M Z       L
            I T E
          H I R D   L I
          S E T I A N Ó Z
            A P E D R Á H C
              E B L O
                E R A
```

---   ------   ---------

----   ------   --------

-----   -------   --------

-----   ------   -------

------   --------

------   --------

Puzzle 60: Room for Growth

Show off your green thumb by filling in the Spanish words for the following words associated with plants, trees, and flowers in the crossword grid. Plant all the words in their correct spaces for a full bloom.

Across

3 CARNATION

6 TREE

8 EVERGREEN OAK

9 GARDEN

10 LAWN

11 PANSY

15 LEAF

16 GROVE

18 ROSE

19 THISTLE

20 POPLAR

21 PLANT

22 SUNFLOWER

26 BUSH/SHRUB

30 LILY

31 ORCHID

Down

1 TULIP

2 IVY

4 VIOLET

5 PINE

7 ASH (TREE)

11 PALM (TREE)

12 JUNGLE/RAIN FOREST

13 DAISY

14 FLOWER

15 GRASS

16 POPPY

17 BIRCH

23 DECIDUOUS OAK

24. SEED

25 ORCHARD

27 FOREST

28 WILLOW

29 ELM

Puzzle 61: Menagerie

Twenty-nine animals appear in the word search grid below. Find all of them, and the remaining letters spell out, in order, a two-word phrase that refers to another place where you might find animals. What is it?

```
O J E N O C P A L P R Q
U O T I G R E O Á E A E
C B R O E Z R J T C Ó T
A O O A R O A E O A O N
B L O N T R N F P B A A
A L D E O Ó O I O R J F
L V A L R Z N Z H A E E
L A N L T A E O A C V L
O C E A U Ó T P N O O E
N A V B G G I A A T O C
O G I R A F A S R A S C
M M U R C I É L A G O O
```

BAT	ELEPHANT	MOLE	TIGER
BEAR	FISH	MONKEY	TOAD
BIRD	FOX	MOUSE	TURTLE
BULL	FROG	PIG	WHALE
CAT	GIRAFFE	RABBIT	WOLF
COW	GOAT	RAT	
DEER	HORSE	SEAL	
DOG	LION	SHEEP	

Puzzle 62: Bugging Out

Translate the 13 Spanish words for types of insects into their English equivalents and then enter them into the grid below. More than one word may fit in any particular space, but the overall solution is unique.

Hint: The words are grouped by the number of letters in their English translation. Don't include articles in the translations.

3 Letters
LA ABEJA
LA HORMIGA
LA MOSCA

4 Letters
LA AVISPA
LA PULGA

5 Letters
EL PIOJO

6 Letters
EL ESCARABAJO

7 Letters
EL GRILLO
LA MARIQUITA

9 Letters
LA CUCARACHA
LA LIBÉLULA
LA MARIPOSA

11 Letters
EL SALTAMONTES

Puzzle 63: It's Elementary

Many of the puzzles in this book explore the world around us, but this one breaks down our environment to its most basic level — the elements. The grid contains 39 chemistry-related terms including 28 well-known elements. When you've found them all, the remaining 22 letters spell out, in order, a two-word phrase that describes how elements might be categorized. What is it?

Puzzle 64: International Geographic

This word search deals with the world around you — literally. Find the names for geographical and topographical features. You may recognize some of them as parts of place names, such as PUERTO in Puerto Rico, which means "rich port" or VEGA in Las Vegas, which means "treeless, empty plain." After you find all the words in the grid, you can find out more translations — as well as the solution grid — in Chapter 10.

```
A L O N G I T U D E S I E R T O Q U A T M
N O V L L A N U R A O I R E F S I M E H A
U C H O O U S U C O C R Á T E R A R F O T
O A R G L P T E R R E M O T O G R R A Á E
O S I L N C E R R O O R R O A I C A I E M
R Í A R T Ó Á O A V E U C N T E R A L L B
A G R P O A Ñ N E Ñ F C É O R R O F A L L
O L L O D D R A D A R I R G E A D N O A O
O N M R A A A D C O C I P I P U N T A V R
G A A P E R N U E R O A T E S E M G E E Í
R L V É E A O E C I P U E R T O A U A A C
N I A E C Ñ R H R E P R E S A T Q L Y O E
Ó A Ñ O G O A R C A S C A D A I S A R T D
L L A A Y A I S E E M J F R D I L D N E U
L L A O R R O M C I R O A G L P I E V R T
A I R A Í H A B P O S T L A Z L I R F R I
R R M C H A R C A A A R S N L R A A L A T
A O C U M B R E R C C A V E R N A N S Z A
F C O I R Ó C O L I N A R O N Ó C J O A L
O I C I P I C E R P R A C M O N T A Ñ A E
L A G U N A M I Z M O N T E O R A T S O C
```

ARENA	ESTRECHO	PASO
ARROYO	FARALLÓN	PEÑASCO
BAHÍA	FOSA	PICO
CABO	HEMISFERIO	PIEDRA
CAÑÓN	ISLA	PLAYA
CASCADA	LADERA	POLO
CATARATA	LAGO	PRECIPICIO
CAVERNA	LAGUNA	PUERTO
CERRO	LATITUD	PUNTA
CHARCA	LLANO	REPRESA
CIÉNAGA	LLANURA	RÍO
CIMA	LOMA	ROCA
COLINA	LONGITUD	SIERRA
CORDILLERA	MAR	TEMBLOR
CORRIENTE	MESETA	TERRAZA
COSTA	MONTAÑA	TERREMOTO
CRÁTER	MONTE	TERRITORIO
CUEVA	MORRO	TIERRA
CUMBRE	OCÉANO	VALLE
DESIERTO	OLA	VEGA
DIQUE	ONDA	VOLCÁN
ECUADOR	ORILLA	

Chapter 7

Travel

Puzzle 65: Currency Exchange

The names of national currencies in the Spanish-speaking world are hidden in the following sentences, indicated by a dollar sign. Using the word list that follows the puzzle, determine where each type of currency fits. Find the name of the currency, and then match it with the name of the country in which that currency is used.

Hint: The name of the currency may straddle more than one word.

1. Will you be able to figure out all the answers to this puzzle? I ho$!
   __PESO (I hoPE SO)__   __MÉXICO__

2. A gon$ide is an enjoyable way to travel around Venice.

3. Mascarpone cheese is what makes tirami$amy.

4. Louis Past$riginated the process of killing microbes in milk.

5. Fillings for a strom$y from pepperoni to spinach.

6. In ancient Rome, Hanni$sted of his military leadership.

7. The proto$ greeting a king or queen is to bow or curtsy to them.

8. Because he had only four years in the Senate, the voting re$ma left before he became president was fairly sparse.

Word List	EURO	EL SALVADOR
BALBOA	~~PESO~~	ESPAÑA
BOLÍVAR	SUCRE	~~MÉXICO~~
COLÓN	*Country List*	NICARAGUA
CÓRDOBA	BOLIVIA	PANAMÁ
DÓLAR	COSTA RICA	VENEZUELA

Puzzle 66: Checking In

Whether you stay at a bed-and-breakfast (*una pensión*), an inn (*una posada*), a hotel (*un hotel*), or a hostel (*un albergue*), you encounter certain words in your living quarters when you travel. Forty-four Spanish words regarding things you might find in a hotel appear on the following page; translate them and find their English equivalents in the word-search grid. And enjoy your stay!

```
N O I T P E C E R I A H C M R A L Y W
F A W E G R E I C N O C D E S K E R E
M V A C H E C K R O O M G N A K T K G
O M K J L T Y B V W B A E T L Y Z G A
O P E B K S S U S S N N E U A A S J G
R A U T H I P T G A I C T O R W U S G
I O P I H G E O M L I A I K M A I D U
D S C T E E A H H V I R U C C L T T L
C K A N H R V Z R L R T S E L L C L L
T B L S O P N E Z S L H B H O O A T U
T E L E V I S I O N S E T C C R S O S
R K T S Z M T K N I S R B E K W E W S
H E T A O Z Y A J I N E B C L O S E T
I A F O R T Y F V U G W D I L L P L S
Y Q R S E T A V I R P O Z O R L O I E
D O O R M A N I K C E H C V P I R B U
P L S S F E L G N I S S R N Z P T D G
M O O P M A H S R A C K E I B Y E V X
C T E L E P H O N E X Y W R Y B R M G
```

ALMOHADA	MALETA
BAÑO	MANTA
BOTONES	PERMANECER
CAMA	PORTAEQUIPAJES
CAMA RODANTE	PORTERO
CHAMPÚ	PRIVADO
CONSERJE	RECEPCIÓN
CONSIGNA	REGISTRARSE
CRIADA	REGISTRO
DESPERTADOR	RESERVA
DOBLE	ROPA BLANCA
DUCHA	ROPERO
EQUIPAJE	SÁBANAS
ESCRITORIO	SENCILLO
FACTURA	SERVICIO DE DESPERTADOR
GERENTE/GERENTA	SERVICIO DE HABITACIÓN
HABITACIÓN	SILLÓN
HÚESPED/HÚESPEDA	SUITE
IRSE	TARIFA
JABÓN	TELEVISOR
LAVABO	TELÉFONO
LLAVE	TOALLA

Puzzle 67: Driving Test

Pass your driving test by unscrambling the letters in the following words, all of which commonly appear on road signs. We give you the English equivalents to help you navigate this puzzle.

1. POTE = TOPE (speed bump)

2. TOLA

3. VUCRA

4. JEAPE

5. NECTOR

6. LADIAS

7. GRILOPE

8. SEPONTEA

9. IPESCADO

10. NIS DALIAS

11. DACE LE SOPA

12. ONZA ED GRACA

13. DESTION ONICÚ

14. STAVI ED STÉINER

15. DAVELOCID AXÁMIM

16. CARREFRIELOSR

17. APARDA ED SÚBAUTO

18. MINACO DORRACE

19. EPUTEN DAZILEVO

20. ADENTRA PHARODIBI

21. ENCASIONETAMITO

22. MAGENTAN US CHERADE

23. NAMETANG US QUIZADIRE

24. PHIDOBIRO BRACIMA ED NOTIDES

25. PHIBORODI BOLARD A AL ARCHEDE

26. HOBODRIPI ALDROB A AL DAIQURIZE

BUS STOP	NO RIGHT TURN
CURVE	NO U-TURN
DANGER	ONE-WAY STREET
DEAD END	PARKING
DO NOT ENTER	PEDESTRIANS
DOWNTOWN	RAILROAD CROSSING
DRAWBRIDGE	ROAD CLOSED
EXIT	SLOW
KEEP LEFT	~~SPEED BUMP~~
KEEP RIGHT	SPEED LIMIT
LOADING ZONE	STOP
LOOKOUT POINT	TOLL
NO LEFT TURN	YIELD

Puzzle 68: Car Trip

You won't need *un GPS* to successfully navigate this puzzle. Translate the 33 words associated with car travel from English to their Spanish equivalents and enter them into the grid. More than one word may fill in any particular space, but the overall solution is unique.

Hint: The words are grouped by the number of letters in their Spanish translation. Don't include articles in the translations.

3 Letters
SOUTH

4 Letters
AUTOMOBILE
EAST
ROUTE

5 Letters
CAR (2 entries)
NORTH
RIDE
STOP (VERB)
STREET
WEST

6 Letters
DETOUR
DRIVER
GARAGE
LANE
ROAD
STOP (NOUN)

7 Letters
AVENUE
DRIVE (VERB)
RIGHT (DIRECTION)
SIGN
STRAIGHT AHEAD

8 Letters
DRIVE (VERB)
PASSENGER
PICK UP (VERB) (2 words)
TRAFFIC LIGHT

9 Letters
AUTOMOBILE
HIGHWAY
LEFT (DIRECTION)
SPEED

10 Letters
GAS STATION

11 Letters
PAVED
REVERSE (2 words)

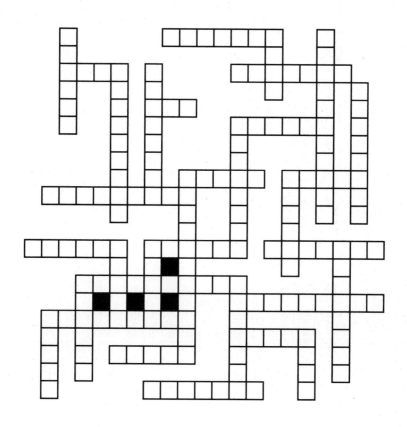

Puzzle 69: Station Identification

There's nothing like a good puzzle to keep you engaged while waiting for your bus or train. In this puzzle, unscramble the following letter strings to form Spanish words and phrases for things you might find in a bus or train depot or words related to bus or train travel. We provide a list of English translations to guide you.

1. AVÍ = VÍA (track)

2. FAIL

3. COBAN

4. DÉNNA

5. GÓVAN

6. JOREL

7. LÚTEN

8. RAILS

9. SLEÑA

10. TRADE

11. VEJIA

12. BOVALA

13. CAMION

14. DALIAS

15. GALLER

16. JAPESA

17. JAVIRA

18. PÉXERS

19. APERRES

20. COQUIOS

21. DAGELLA

22. JOVERIA

23. GÓNVA MODERCO

24. ORAHORI

25. PILLOSA

26. RETOREL

27. SEATION

28. SABÚTUO

29. SORRATE

30. TEBLIEL

31. UNIONCA

32. ZALOTAV

33. PORTNAME

34. QUEJAPIE

35. JOSEPARA

36. ROARG JARO

37. HECCO-ACAM

38. COLAROTOMO

39. SOPA A LIVEN

40. PAJEIQUE ED NOMA

41. LASA ED PESARE

42. QUITALLA ED AVENT

43. RIOCART ED JAPEQUIE

44. SETACA ED MANÓRIFICON

45. INÓTESCA ED SÚBOTUA

46. ASECTIÓN ED REFORRLICRA

47. TALA LECODIVAD PESOLAÑA

AISLE

ANNOUNCEMENT

ARRIVAL

ARRIVE

AVE TRAIN
(high-speed rail
system in Spain)

BENCH

BUS

BUS STATION

CARRY-ON BAG

CLOCK

DELAY

DEPART

DEPARTURE

DINING CAR

EARLY

EXPRESS

FARE

INFORMATION
BOOTH

LATE

LAVATORY

LEVEL CROSSING

LOCOMOTIVE

LOUDSPEAKER

LUGGAGE

LUGGAGE CART

NEWSSTAND

PASSENGER

PLATFORM

RAILROAD CAR

REDCAP

ROAD

ROW

SCHEDULE

SEAT

SIGN

SIGNAL

SLEEPING CAR

TICKET

TICKET COUNTER

~~TRACK~~

TRAIN STATION

TRAVEL (VERB)

TRAVELER

TRIP

TUNNEL

WAIT (VERB)

WAITING ROOM

Puzzle 70: Mechanical Engineering

Most people don't think much about their cars until some part needs fixing, and then they usually just call the mechanic. But being able to identify the parts of an automobile is still important. Can you find the Spanish words for 34 parts of a car hidden in this word search diagram?

Hint: Most of the words run horizontally, but six run diagonally and three are positioned vertically.

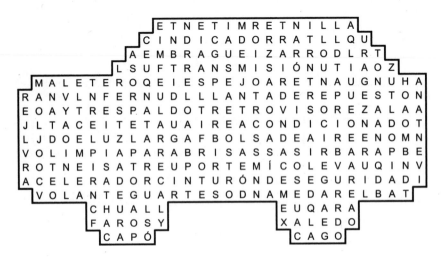

```
        E T N E T I M R E T N I L L A
        C I N D I C A D O R R A T L L Q U
        A E M B R A G U E I Z A R R O D L R T
        L S U F T R A N S M I S I Ó N U T I A O Z
M A L E T E R O Q E I E S P E J O A R E T N A U G N U H A
R A N V L N F E R N U D L L L A N T A D E R E P U E S T O N
E O A Y T R E S P A L D O T R E T R O V I S O R E Z A L A A
J L T A C E I T E T A U A I R E A C O N D I C I O N A D O T
L J D O E L U Z L A R G A F B O L S A D E A I R E E N O M N
V O L I M P I A P A R A B R I S A S S A S I R B A R A P B E
R O T N E I S A T R E U P O R T E M Í C O L E V A U Q I N V
A C E L E R A D O R C I N T U R Ó N D E S E G U R I D A D I
V O L A N T E G U A R T E S O D N A M E D A R E L B A T
        C H U A L L           E U Q A R A
        F A R O S Y           X A L E D O
        C A P Ó               C A G O
```

Puzzle 71: National Pastime

This word game may be countrified, but the answers are clever and sophisticated! Answer the following word riddles about the names of Spanish-speaking countries. You won't use all of the countries listed, but you won't repeat any, either.

The name of what Spanish-speaking country

1. Becomes a Spanish word for a beverage when its last two letters are moved to the front, and its last letter changed to another vowel?

2. Becomes a woman's name when its first letter is removed?

3. Becomes a Spanish word for something you might see in a rainstorm when its last letter is changed?

4. Contains hidden in its name, in consecutive order, letters that can spell the Spanish word for a part of the body?

5. Can be coded as a cryptogram for the English word ELEMENT?

6. Becomes an English word for a type of fruit when either its first or last letter is changed and the result is anagrammed?

7. Becomes the Spanish word for an occupation when its third letter is changed?

8. Becomes an English word meaning "wholesome" when its two vowels are switched?

9. Becomes an English word for a numeral when its sixth letter is changed and the new letter string is unscrambled?

10. Can form an English word that can form another English word when its letters are reversed when either vowel is removed?

ARGENTINA	HONDURAS
BOLIVIA	MEXICO
CHILE	NICARAGUA
COLOMBIA	PANAMA
COSTA RICA	PARAGUAY
CUBA	PERU
DOMINICAN REPUBLIC	PUERTO RICO
ECUADOR	SPAIN
EL SALVADOR	URUGUAY
GUATEMALA	VENEZUELA

Puzzle 72: What's in a Name?

You find Spanish place names not only in Spain and South and Central America, but right here in the United States. Translate the English meanings and derivations below into their Spanish equivalents and then enter them in the grid. More than one name may fit a particular entry, but the overall solution is unique.

5 Letters

TILES

6 Letters

ASH TREE
BIG EARS
LIVE OAK
SNOWY
THE PASS (2 words)
TOWN

7 Letters

FLOWERY
HOLY FAITH (2 words)
MODEST
MOUNTAIN
SAINT JOSEPH (2 words)
SALT MARSHES

8 Letters

KING'S MOUNTAIN
RED
SAINT JAMES (2 words)
TALL TREE (2 words)
TREELESS, EMPTY PLAINS
   (2 words)
YELLOW

9 Letters

GREEN BUTTE (2 words)
HOLY CROSS (2 words)
THE CROSSES (2 words)

10 Letters

BIG POPLAR
OAK PASS (2 words)
SACRAMENT
THE ANGELS (2 words)

11 Letters

MOTHER RANGE (2 words)

12 Letters

SAINT FRANCIS (2 words)

14 Letters

BLOOD OF CHRIST (3 words)

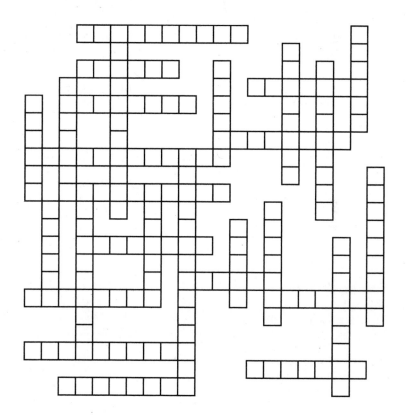

Puzzle 73: National Spelling Bee

Using the English translations as a guide, decode the Spanish names of these 29 countries in the non-Spanish-speaking world. Note that some Spanish country names contain articles but don't necessarily have "the" in their English names; the articles are included in parentheses if they are required in Spanish.

Hint: No countries in this puzzle have the same spellings in Spanish and English, so you won't find nations such as Australia, Austria, China, India, or Israel.

1. (DG) KBEIFG =
   (EL) BRASIL

2. FJEGFE

3. BNIFE

4. MBDWFE

5. YUGUTFE

6. FTMGEJDBBE

7. ZBETWFE

8. INXEZBFWE

9. JNBANFE

10. GUI DIJEXUI NTFXUI

11. EZMETFIJET

12. EGDRETFE

13. (DG) WETEXE

14. GEI ZFGFYFTEI

15. JEFGETXFE

16. YEANFIJET

17. DIWUWFE

18. DMFYJU

19. EBEKFE IENXFJE

20. TUBNDME

21. FBGETXE

22. FBEH

23. (DG) CEYUT

24. HDTFE

25. INDWFE

26. MEGDI

27. ZFTGETXFE

28. CUBXETFE

29. XFTEREBWE

AFGHANISTAN	KENYA
~~BRAZIL~~	NORWAY
CANADA	PAKISTAN
DENMARK	THE PHILIPPINES
EGYPT	POLAND
ENGLAND	RUSSIA
FINLAND	SAUDI ARABIA
FRANCE	SCOTLAND
GERMANY	SOUTH AFRICA
GREECE	SWEDEN
IRAQ	THAILAND
IRELAND	TURKEY
ITALY	THE UNITED STATES
JAPAN	WALES
JORDAN	

Puzzle 74: Jet Set

If you fly to a Spanish-speaking country to practice the Spanish you're learning in this book, you'll find the vocabulary related to air travel extremely useful. We've hidden 46 of these words in the grid below. Based on their English translations, can you find them all?

```
S E N C I L L O D E I D A Y V U E L T A C A B
X A O O A L A C S E N I S A P A S A J E R O R
P I D E S E M B A R C A R S E T B Q R A A E D
C I E A R E R A Z A L O D D S B E A C Z X Q E
I P L J R V G O U R M M R L E I J R A E R U M
N P A O A P D I P E E A A J B A U F M U H A A
T E X S T S L E D U T M A L B X A X H I C N N
U D E B A O A E H R E P P L E T A S I E N T O
R O S O D P L P P G I R Q U A T F T O E R A M
Ó M R L O M O U A U R I T E C U A Z S S S A L
N R A E S C E R Q E R I G O O D L E E I T L R
D A C T A R J E T A D E E M B A R Q U E P L A
E R R O T Y E L B E M E L C O S S A O L O I Z
S U A A A Q O L E U V E D R A I L I X U A N I
E T B L B O T Ó N D E L L A M A D A R R I A R
G C M C O N T R O L D E S E G U R I D A D T R
U A E B A V S A L I D A O Z R S O R E D R N E
R F B B I L L E T E R P N L D U P E R A L E T
I I R Q E P G C O R M L Ó E L B R O D Z E V A
D N L V I A J A R E R T I L R I E O R I L D C
A T E A D A R L I V E L V D I R S T A J E S P
D H M A S E N T A R S E A A O I R A R O H O H
A B R O C H A R S E E A T Z R A G E P S E D T
```

AIRPLANE
AIRPORT
AIRSICKNESS
AISLE
ARRIVAL
BAGGAGE/LUGGAGE
BOARD (VERB) (2 entries)
BOARDING PASS (3 words)
CALL BUTTON (3 words)
CARRY-ON (ADJECTIVE)
   (2 words)
CHECK (BAGGAGE)
DEPLANE (2 entries)
DELAY (NOUN)
EXIT (NOUN)

FASTEN
FLIGHT ATTENDANT
   (3 words)
FLY (VERB)
GATE
LAND (VERB)
LATE
LEAVE (VERB)
NONSTOP (2 words)
ON TIME (2 words)
ONE-WAY
PASSENGER
PASSPORT
PILOT (NOUN)
ROUND TRIP (4 words)

RUNWAY
SCHEDULE (NOUN)
SEAT (NOUN)
SEAT BELT (3 words)
SECURITY AREA (3 words)
SIT
STEWARDESS
SUITCASE
TAKE OFF (VERB)
TERMINAL
TICKET (3 entries)
TRAVEL (VERB)
WINDOW
WING

Chapter 8

The Spanish World: Culture, Geography, and History

● ●

Puzzle 75: Local Flavor

Decode the common dishes listed next to the country and territory names where they're served. We hope this puzzle whets your appetite enough to try some of these foods in a restaurant or in your own kitchen.

Hint: We put some of the more common dishes at the beginning of the list. The list is divided into two sections — the first 14 and the last 21 — each of which is in alphabetical order.

1. HDDQY   <u>   ARROZ   </u>

2. KFDDOVQJ   <u>   </u>

3. NWOGONWHPMHJ   <u>   </u>

4. TGCHPHSHJ   <u>   </u>

5. TPNWOAHSHJ (ARGENTINA)   <u>   </u>

6. UHLOVHJ   <u>   </u>

7. UDOLQATJ   <u>   </u>

8. MFHNHGQAT   <u>   </u>

9. GQAT   <u>   </u>

10. CHTAAH   <u>   </u>

11. CONQ ST MHAAQ   <u>   </u>

12. VHNQJ   <u>   </u>

13. VHGHATJ _____

14. VHCHJ (SPAIN) _____

15. HLOHNQ (COLOMBIA, CUBA) _____

16. HDTCHJ _____

17. HDDQY NQP MHPSFATJ (PUERTO RICO) _____

18. KHPSTLH CHOJH (COLOMBIA) _____

19. NHDPT HJHSH _____

20. NHYFTAH (CHILE) _____

21. NTEONWT (ECUADOR, PERU, PANAMA) _____

22. NWOEOVQ (URUGUAY) _____

23. NFI (ANDEAN COUNTRIES) _____

24. MHAAQ COPVQ (COSTA RICA, NICARAGUA, PANAMA)
    _____

25. WFGOPVHJ (BOLIVIA) _____

26. LOKHDOVQJ (PUERTO RICO) _____

27. ATNWQP _____

28. GQDQJ I NDOJVOHPQJ (CUBA) _____

29. CHKTAAQP (DOMINICAN REPUBLIC, VENEZUELA)
    _____

30. CHDDOAAHSH _____

31. CFCFJHJ (EL SALVADOR) _____

32. JHPNQNWQ (COLOMBIA, PANAMA) _____

33. JTDDHPQ (SPAIN) _____

34. VHNQJ HA CHJVQD (MEXICO) _____

35. VHCHSQ (GUATEMALA) _____

Puzzle 76: South American Way

Do your own search in the Land of El Dorado and circle the names of all 13 Latin American countries hidden within. Look for an extra feature in this word map.

Hint: One country has a two-word name, and each part is entered separately, so you are looking for 14 words in total.

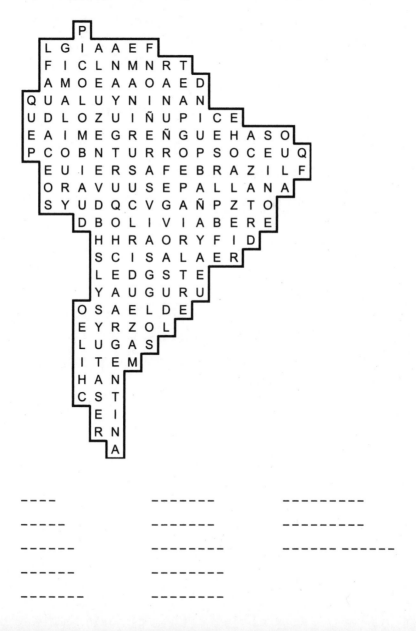

```
        P
   L G I A A E F
   F I C L N M N R T
   A M O E A A O A E D
 Q U A L U Y N I N A N
 U D L O Z U I Ñ U P I C E
 E A I M E G R E Ñ G U E H A S O
 P C O B N T U R R O P S O C E U Q
   E U I E R S A F E B R A Z I L F
   O R A V U U S E P A L L A N A
   S Y U D Q C V G A Ñ P Z T O
       D B O L I V I A B E R E
       H H R A O R Y F I D
       S C I S A L A E R
       L E D G S T E
       Y A U G U R U
     O S A E L D E
     E Y R Z O L
     L U G A S
     I T E M
     H A N
     C S T
       E I
       R N
         A
```

_ _ _ _   _ _ _ _ _ _   _ _ _ _ _ _ _ _ _

_ _ _ _ _   _ _ _ _ _ _   _ _ _ _ _ _ _ _

_ _ _ _ _ _   _ _ _ _ _ _ _   _ _ _ _ _ _ _ _ _ _ _

_ _ _ _ _ _   _ _ _ _ _ _ _

_ _ _ _ _ _ _   _ _ _ _ _ _ _

Puzzle 77: Hall of Fame

To win your solving trophy, unscramble the names of the 15 famous people from the Spanish-speaking world. The names appear in three groups of five each. After you have the names within each group, place the letters with numbers under them in order to reveal the occupation that all the members of that group share.

1. LIUMGE ED VSTECAREN _ _ _ _ _ _ _ _ _ _ _ _ _ _ _ _ _

            2   1

2. GERJO SLIU REBOSG _ _ _ _ _ _ _ _ _ _ _ _ _ _

           4   5

3. NTOUJ ZÍDA _ _ _ _ _ _ _ _ _

          3

4. DOÁCLIP GODOMNI _ _ _ _ _ _ _ _ _ _ _ _ _ _

           2   3

5. SÉJO ARRESCAR _ _ _ _ _ _ _ _ _ _ _

         8 1 5

6. TERRAMONTS LÉBACAL _ _ _ _ _ _ _ _ _ _ _ _ _ _ _ _ _

           6 4   7

7. ENPLOPÉE ZURC _ _ _ _ _ _ _ _ _ _ _ _

             2   6

8. MALAS KEYHA _ _ _ _ _ _ _ _ _ _

        1

9. TARI ROMONE _ _ _ _ _ _ _ _ _ _

       5 3   4

10. ORTENES "HÉC" VARGUEA _ _ _ _ _ _ _ "_ _ _" _ _ _ _ _ _ _

                   14   6 11 1

11. FIELD ACTORS _ _ _ _ _ _ _ _ _ _

        13 2   7   124

12. CHOPAN LIVAL _ _ _ _ _ _ _ _ _ _ _

         10   9 3 8 5

13. ROTBELA ALARZAS _ _ _ _ _ _ _ _ _ _ _ _ _

           5   6

14. BOTEROR MELENCET _ _ _ _ _ _ _ _ _ _ _ _ _ _ _

           4   3

15. EVES TOBALESERLS _ _ _ _ _ _ _ _ _ _ _ _ _

          1   2

Puzzle 78: Round Up the Usual Suspects

While Hispanics have made many important contributions throughout history, they are also well-represented in literature, theater, opera, television, and movies. See if you can find all 19 fictional characters hidden in the grid below. If you're successful, that's a real accomplishment.

```
L Z E H C N Á S O R D E P W A Z
S E L A Z N O G Y D E E P S O E
S S D I K O C S I C E H T R T N
R E R O L P X E E H T A R O D É
P Y A K Z Y C V N V U O A S O M
D E N R I Q U E M U N I Z O N I
U R W U P Z F R X T I F N T Q J
L Y L H Y O O I T G U B A N U É
C E Z N S S L C G J L N P A I S
I L A T I C Z L G A O H O S X O
N R N T A F W M I Q R R H T O J
E U A R D W O X N M D O C T T H
A H M N A U J N O D A N N A E E
G E Y T T E B Y L G U C A M X K
N L K L W X U Q U X I N S O M A
A B L A A D R A N R E B P E O T
```

_ _ _ _ _   _ _ _ _ _ _ _   _ _ _ _ _ _ _ _

_ _ _ _ _ _   _ _ _ _ _ _ _   _ _ _ _ _ _ _ _

_ _ _ _ _   _ _ _ _ _ _ _   _ _ _ _ _ _ _ _

_ _ _ _ _   _ _ _ _ _ _ _ _ _   _ _ _ _ _ _ _ _ _ _

_ _ _ _ _ _ _   _ _ _ _ _ _ _ _ _   _ _ _ _ _ _ _ _ _ _ _

_ _ _ _ _ _ _   _ _ _ _ _ _ _ _

_ _ _ _ _ _   _ _ _ _ _ _ _ _ _

Puzzle 79: Capital Letters

Place in the grid the Spanish names of the countries and territories that correspond to their capitals in the clues below.

Across

3 México D.F.
5 Ciudad de Panamá
6 Lima
8 Santiago
11 San José
12 Madrid
13 Bogotá
16 Quito
17 Buenos Aires
18 Asunción
19 Ciudad de Guatemala

Down

1 Tegucigalpa
2 Santo Domingo
4 San Juan
7 Managua
9 Caracas
10 San Salvador
11 La Habana
14 La Paz (administrative)/Sucre (constitutional/judicial)
15 Montevideo

Puzzle 80: Turns of Phrase

This puzzle tests whether a word to the wise is sufficient and whether you really do learn something new every day. Unscramble each of the words below to form a Spanish proverb or saying. Then match each with its English equivalent. As an added challenge, these phrases do not translate word-for-word from Spanish to English, so you have to use a little more brainpower to figure them out.

1. ROPE SE ADAN. = PEOR ES NADA.

2. VESPERARE Y SIFUNTIRRÁ.

3. NE LIBRA, SAGAU LMI.

4. A LAM PETIMO, NEBUA ACAR.

5. LE UEQ ON ROLLA, ON AMAM.

6. TERNE SUBEYE ON YAH SODACARN.

7. DUNACO AHY BREHMA, ON YHA NAP ODUR.

8. ARÍC VUSCERO Y ET NÁRACAS SOL JOSO.

9. SENTA EQU ET SECAS, MARI OL EUQ SACHE.

10. ON ES NÓGA MORAZA NE ANU RAHO.

11. SOJO QEU ON NEV, NAZÓRCO EQU ON LARLO.

12. LED HICOD LA CHEHO, YAH CHUMO OTCHER.

~~HALF A LOAF IS BETTER THAN NONE.~~	TALK IS CHEAP.
	NEVER SAY DIE.
APRIL SHOWERS BRING MAY FLOWERS.	OUT OF SIGHT, OUT OF MIND.
THERE IS NO HONOR AMONG THIEVES.	LET A SMILE BE YOUR UMBRELLA.
LIE DOWN WITH DOGS AND YOU WAKE UP WITH FLEAS.	THE SQUEAKY WHEEL GETS THE GREASE.
ROME WASN'T BUILT IN A DAY.	LOOK BEFORE YOU LEAP.
BEGGARS CAN'T BE CHOOSERS.	

Puzzle 81: Keeping the Faith

We believe you can complete this crossword without too much difficulty, but please don't solve it in your house of worship! Enter the Spanish translations of the following English religious terminology in the grid.

Across

2 CROSS

4 BIBLE

6 CHURCH

7 SERMON

8 ALTAR BOY

10 WORSHIPPERS/
 CONGREGANTS

12 KORAN

13 FUNERAL

16 BELIEVER

19 FRIAR

20 MUHAMMAD

21 ISLAM

23 CRESCENT

24 PRAYER

25 MOSES

27 IMAM

28 TEMPLE

29 CHOIR

30 SYNAGOGUE

Down

1 PASTOR

2 PRIEST

3 JESUS CHRIST

5 STAR OF DAVID

9 MONK

11 DIOCESE

12 CATHEDRAL

14 RABBI

15 MOSQUE

17 CHRISTIANITY

18 JUDAISM

20 MINISTER

22 ABRAHAM

23 MASS

24 BISHOP

25 NUN

26 WEDDING

Puzzle 82: The Natives Are Restless

Unscramble the following strings of letters to get the nationalities associated with Spanish-speaking countries and territories. When you're finished, the letters in the numbered spaces will spell out, in order, a two-word phrase that may be an alternative title for this puzzle. The countries are listed at the bottom as a guide.

Hint: Because nationalities are adjectives and agree in gender with their subjects, 10 answers have masculine endings and nine have feminine endings. Two of them do not change with gender.

1. EXCAMINO   _ _ _ _ _ _ _
                1

2. DINACAMINO   _ _ _ _ _ _ _ _ _
         2

3. MAÑAPANE   _ _ _ _ _ _ _ _
                3

4. EUROPAN   _ _ _ _ _ _ _
                4

5. HELICAN   _ _ _ _ _ _ _

6. ANGERTION   _ _ _ _ _ _ _ _ _
                5

7. OBLIVIONA   _ _ _ _ _ _ _ _ _
            6

8. ACUEORATION   _ _ _ _ _ _ _ _ _ _ _
            7

9. UYOAGURU   _ _ _ _ _ _ _ _
                8

10. AUPRAYOGA   _ _ _ _ _ _ _ _ _

11. BINOCALOMA   _ _ _ _ _ _ _ _ _ _
         9

12. UNBACA   _ _ _ _ _ _

13. DOÑARNUHE   _ _ _ _ _ _ _ _ _
                10

14. ANLOVEZONE   _ _ _ _ _ _ _ _ _ _

15. QUITAREÑUPERRO   _ _ _ _ _ _ _ _ _ _ _ _ _
                                        11

16. DOÑALOVERSA   _ _ _ _ _ _ _ _ _ _

17. POLEÑASA   _ _ _ _ _ _ _ _
                         12

18. GENUAIATANOUCE   _ _ _ _ _ _ _ _ _ _ _ _ _

19. CARINGESÜENA   _ _ _ _ _ _ _ _ _ _ _
                         13

20. GALETAMACUTE   _ _ _ _ _ _ _ _ _ _ _

21. CARRESECTIONS   _ _ _ _ _ _ _ _ _ _ _
                                14

LA ARGENTINA	ESPAÑA	EL PARAGUAY
BOLIVIA	GUATEMALA	EL PERÚ
CHILE	GUINEA ECUATORIAL	PUERTO RICO
COLOMBIA	HONDURAS	LA REPÚBLICA DOMINICANA
COSTA RICA	MÉXICO	EL URUGUAY
CUBA	NICARAGUA	VENEZUELA
EL ECUADOR	PANAMÁ	
EL SALVADOR		

Puzzle 83: When in Roma . . .

You may know that a New Yorker is *un neoyorquino* in Spanish or that a Parisian is *un parisiense,* but do you know the terms for natives of various cities and territories in Spanish-speaking countries? Twenty-five are hidden in this grid; many of them share similar roots from their locations of origin, but some differ quite considerably.

Hint: Eleven of the adjectives are feminine, 12 are masculine, and two are unisex.

```
C O N A I C E N E V O T O A B C C
A Í Q S É B O D R O C G S B A H H
R T O L E D A N A Z E E G U N I E
A A O A R R E U Q L N M R R O H S
Q P N S A N O U L O A Í A G M U A
U A A O P L R A L D O N N A L A N
E T L N I H G E R P I Y L L Ñ H I
Ñ N L M É I C I L L O A E E D U D
O D E T C R L A A O G R M S C E A
Q Ñ T Í A E T T N U R E T A S N N
A U S B Ñ E I B E D R E T E A S A
L R A O N P O Ñ V T A A N L Ñ E R
S R C S A Q O U X A L L L A F O G
A O E C T U R E Ó A S I U I B A O
N A C S A V I O N N V O P Z E A N
G U A N T A N A M E R O A R A R H
O N A T O G O B S É N O G A R A T
```

_ _ _ _ _   _ _ _ _ _ _ _ _   _ _ _ _ _ _ _ _ _   _ _ _ _ _ _ _ _ _ _ _

_ _ _ _ _ _   _ _ _ _ _ _ _ _   _ _ _ _ _ _ _ _ _   _ _ _ _ _ _ _ _ _ _ _

_ _ _ _ _ _ _   _ _ _ _ _ _ _ _   _ _ _ _ _ _ _ _ _   _ _ _ _ _ _ _ _ _ _ _

_ _ _ _ _ _ _   _ _ _ _ _ _ _ _   _ _ _ _ _ _ _ _ _   _ _ _ _ _ _ _ _ _ _ _

_ _ _ _ _ _   _ _ _ _ _ _ _ _   _ _ _ _ _ _ _ _ _

_ _ _ _ _ _ _ _   _ _ _ _ _ _ _ _ _   _ _ _ _ _ _ _ _ _

_ _ _ _ _ _ _ _   _ _ _ _ _ _ _ _ _   _ _ _ _ _ _ _ _ _

Puzzle 84: Lost in Translation

Rearrange the letters in each of the individual Spanish words to form correct film titles. The original English titles are provided below, and the first one is done to get you started.

Hint: Not all of the new titles are exact word-for-word translations; for those you may want to look for synonyms to some of the English words to provide context.

1. AL LABEL Y AL TISBEA = LA BELLA Y LA BESTIA

2. SODED ED ROO

3. SEGURRA ED SAL ALIXAGAS

4. SLA VUSA ED AL ARI

5. SHERMBO ED GONER

6. ANUTEC MOCIGNO

7. LE OÑSER ED SLO LANILOS

8. ¡UÉQ LOLEB SE RIVVI!

9. SENUBO CHUSOCHAM

10. SOL ZADORESCA LED CARA DRAPIDE

11. OL EQU LE TEVINO ES VELLÓ

12. OLS JEROMES OÑAS ED NATURES DIVA

BEAUTY AND THE BEAST   IT'S A WONDERFUL LIFE

THE BEST YEARS OF OUR LIVES   THE LORD OF THE RINGS

GOLDFINGER   MEN IN BLACK

GONE WITH THE WIND   RAIDERS OF THE LOST ARK

GOODFELLAS   STAND BY ME

THE GRAPES OF WRATH   STAR WARS

Puzzle 85: Man of La Mancha

Published in the early 17th century, *Don Quijote*, or *El Ingenioso Hidalgo Don Quijote de la Mancha,* by Miguel de Cervantes Saavedra is the most influential work in the Spanish literary canon and arguably one of the most important works in any language. This word search contains some important vocabulary featured in the novel; we provide English translations (or brief descriptions, where appropriate) to help you find the Spanish words in the grid. We hope that this puzzle motivates you to go on your own quest to find the complete novel at your bookstore or library.

```
D O N A Í R E L L A B A C L L
I T A T I É J C A L A N Z A P
N N H D O V E L H J R A A V E
G E I U Y B U Y O F D R N Í T
E I D L I M O R P E F U C X O
N V A C U I E S U G L C A T X
I E L I Q T D Q O M O I B E I
O D G N N B S G A F D O A R U
S O O E S Ú L R X Z U I L E Q
O N V A B P U J N I C H L S N
N I C H A T O F Ó T S E O A O
A L D O N Z A L O R E N Z O D
O O M E S A N C H O P A N Z A
L M V R O C I N A N T E S O R
E A M O R E D U C S E L E N A
```

ADVENTURE

ALDONZA LORENZO (Dulcinea's real name)

CHIVALRY

CLEVER/INGENIOUS/INVENTIVE

DON QUIJOTE (the main character)

DULCINEA (Don Quijote's love)

HORSE

INNKEEPER

KNIGHT ERRANT

LA MANCHA (Don Quijote's homeland)

LANCE

LANDOWNER/NOBLEMAN

MULE

QUEST

ROCINANTE (Don Quijote's horse)

RUCIO (Sancho Panza's donkey)

SANCHO PANZA (Don Quijote's sidekick)

SHIELD

SQUIRE

TERESA (Sancho Panza's wife)

TOBOSO (Dulcinea's hometown, currently a town in the province of Toledo, Spain)

WINDMILL

Puzzle 86: Royal Wedding

The letter fragments below can be "married" in groups of two to form the Spanish words for various titles of nobility. The English equivalents, along with the enumerations of the Spanish words appear at left. Successfully find all the correct pairs and you'll be crowned as an expert solver.

Hint: The solution words are arranged by length starting with the shortest.

1. KING (3)   REY

2. LADY (4)

3. BARON (5)

4. COUNT/EARL (5)

5. LORD (5)

6. NOBLE (5)

7. QUEEN (5)

8. VICEROY (6)

9. COUNTESS (7)

10. ROYALTY (7)

11. BARONESS (8)

12. HEIR (8)

13. PRINCE (8)

14. PRINCESS (8)

15. AMBASSADOR (9)

16. EMPEROR (9)

17. KNIGHT (9)

18. EMPRESS (10)

19. ARISTOCRAT (11)

20. LADY-IN-WAITING (11) (3 words)

~~Y~~	BAR	VIR	LERO	EMBAJ
DA	BLE	ADOR	LEZA	EMPER
DE	CON	BARO	NESA	RADOR
MA	CON	CESA	PRIN	ARISTÓ
ÓN	ESA	CIPE	PRÍN	EHONOR
NA	ÑOR	COND	ATRIZ	
NO	REA	DERO	CABAL	
~~RE~~	REI	EMPE	CRATA	
SE	REY	HERE	DAMAD	

Puzzle 87: Odd One Out

The famous Hispanic men and women in this puzzle have had the letters in their names strung together, and the odd letters removed. Given the string of letters and a brief description, can you identify them? The location of the spaces separating first and last names is for you to determine.

1. EEA (CANTANTE)   _____SELENA_____

2. VPRN (PRIMERA DAMA)   _____

3. ATNLS (ACTOR, CÓMICO)   _____

4. RDKHO (PINTORA)   _____

5. OÉERR (ACTOR)   _____

6. ÉACAE (ACTIVISTA)   _____

7. ALCSL (MÚSICO)   _____

8. EEOCO (CIENTÍFICO, NOBELISTA)   _____

9. IÓBLVR (ESTADISTA)   _____

10. EIOURZ (ESTADISTA)   _____

11. ALPCSO (PINTOR)   _____

12. AVDRAÍ (PINTOR)   _____

13. NRSEOI (GUITARRISTA)   _____

14. UÍEOER (CURA, EXPLORADOR)   _____

15. AOAIAS (DISEÑADORA)   _____

16. RSÓACLN (EXPLORADOR)   _____

17. ERAMDVR (DIRECTOR)   _____

18. ADAINRS (AUTORA)   _____

19. OISTMYR (JURISTA)   _____

20. LOSNSON (POETISA)   _____

21. AOIAERR (DISEÑADORA)   _____

22. AREAITA (POETISA, NOBELISTA)   _____

23. UNOCDLÓ (EXPLORADOR)   _____

24. ORGDADVVR (CABALLERO)   _____

25. RNXSNHZIAI (ATLETA)   _____

Puzzle 88: Arts and Letters

Many people from the Spanish-speaking world have made contributions to the visual arts. In this crossword, each clue contains the first name, discipline, and country of origin of a well-known artisan. Their last names fill the answers in the grid. The one exception is 17 Down, where the answer is the two-word nickname by which this artist is much more famous.

Across

3 PABLO _____, PALOMA _____ (Pintor, Spain; Diseñadora, Spain)

5 BARTOLOMÉ ESTEBAN _____ (Pintor, Spain)

7 FRANCISCO DE _____ (Pintor, Spain)

9 DIEGO DE _____ (Pintor, México)

13 CRISTÓBAL _____ (Diseñador, Spain)

14 JOAN _____ (Pintor, Spain)

15 PACO _____ (Diseñador, Spain)

18 ÓSCAR _____ (Diseñador, Dominican Republic)

19 ADOLFO _____ (Diseñador, Cuba)

20 JOSEP LLUIS _____, JOSEP MARÍA _____ (Arquitecto, Spain; Pintor, Spain)

21 FRIDA _____ (Pintora, México)

Down

1 SALVADOR _____ (Pintor, Spain)

2 SANTIAGO _____ (Arquitecto, Spain)

4 JOSÉ CLEMENTE _____ (Pintor, México)

6 DIEGO _____ (Pintor, México)

8 CAROLINA _____ (Diseñador, Venezuela)

10 FRANCISCO DE _____ (Pintor, Spain)

11 ANTONI _____ (Arquitecto, Spain)

12 DAVID ALFARO _____ (Pintor, México)

16 MANOLO _____ (Diseñador, Spain)

17 DOMÉNIKOS THEOTOKÓPOULOS _____ (Pintor, Spain)

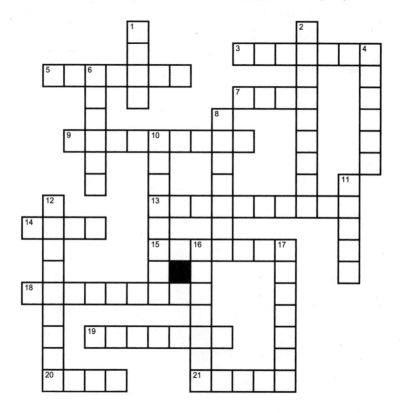

Puzzle 89: Get It in Writing

The names of 16 writers of the Spanish-speaking world appear in code. We list the authors in alphabetical order by last name and give you the name of a famous or representative work and their country of origin in the same order in which they appear on the list.

1. BGCINW CWWNXMN = ISABEL ALLENDE

2. THGECLJ CMJWPJ INKZHNO

3. UJOTN WHBG IJOTNG

4. ABTHNW MN KNOLCXENG GCCLNMOC

5. UHWBJ KJOECSCO

6. OHINX MCOBJ

7. KCOWJG PHNXENG

8. PNMNOBKJ TCOKBC WJOKC

9. TCIOBNW TCOKBC ACOZHNS

10. WJYN MN LNTC

11. UJGN ACOEB

12. YCIWJ XNOHMC

13. JKECLBJ YCS

14. INXBEJ YNONS TCWMJG

15. UHCX OHWPJ

16. ACOBJ LCOTCG WWJGC

LA CASA DE LOS ESPÍRITUS, CHILE

RIMAS, SPAIN

LOS DOS REYES Y LOS DOS LABERINTOS, ARGENTINA

DON QUIJOTE DE LA MANCHA, SPAIN

RAYUELA, ARGENTINA

AZUL, NICARAGUA

LA MUERTE DE ARTEMIO CRUZ, MÉXICO

LA CASA DE BERNARDA ALBA, SPAIN

CIEN AÑOS DE SOLEDAD, COLOMBIA

FUENTEOVEJUNA, SPAIN

VERSOS SENCILLOS, CUBA

VEINTE POEMAS DE AMOR Y UNA CANCIÓN DESESPERADA, CHILE

EL LABERINTO DE LA SOLEDAD, MÉXICO

FORTUNATA Y JACINTA, SPAIN

PEDRO PÁRAMO, MÉXICO

CONVERSACIÓN EN LA CATEDRAL, PERÚ

Puzzle 90: Second Cities

Many people know their capitals, but many other major cities throughout Spain and Latin America are worth knowing. Unscramble these place names and then match them to their home countries and territories from the list.

1. ÓNEL   <u>LEÓN, NICARAGUA</u>

2. ALIC   _____

3. OLNÓC   _____

4. OCCUZ   _____

5. PECON   _____

6. ALTOS   _____

7. GUIANTA   _____

8. DROBÓCA   _____

9. STANA NAA   _____

10. CROLENABA   _____

11. CABO HACCI   _____

12. QUILAGUYA   _____

13. CARAMBAIO   _____

14. CHAMBACOBA   _____

15. PÓNICECOCN   _____

16. AMONGUÁNTA   _____

17. SALVAPORÍA   _____

18. JAGUARADALA   _____

19. RUTOPE MÓLIN   _____

20. ANS DROPE ULAS   _____

ARGENTINA	CUBA	HONDURAS	PERÚ
BOLIVIA	ECUADOR	MÉXICO	PUERTO RICO
CHILE	EL SALVADOR	~~NICARAGUA~~	REPÚBLICA DOMINICANA
COLOMBIA	ESPAÑA	PANAMÁ	URUGUAY
COSTA RICA	GUATEMALA	PARAGUAY	VENEZUELA

Puzzle 91: Strike Up the Band

The Spanish words for 27 musical instruments appear in the grid across, down, and diagonally.

Hint: The instruments that appear in the grid are located in their approximate location in a diagram of a standard orchestra — strings on the left and right sides, woodwinds near the front (at the bottom of the grid), and percussion and brass instruments near the back (at the top).

```
A S T E R Í N A T E N R O C T T C
M L O A C H E C A T E P M O R T Í
A D O L M A Z A C E D O N R O C T
N A N L L B A F P Á R E R O M I A
D P O P S T O G I L Ó R P E B D R
O R F L A R F R A R R E L L Ó A A
L A Á A L A C E N E T U B A N C V
I G R T E N Ó F O X A S E H C O I
N U B I U G O N A G R Ó E A O S O
A I I L Ñ A Ñ U R A C T O U N A L
N T V L A L E S E L E A D S T Í O
Í A P O T E A Z O N E Z E Ú R E N
L R O S S C L E I C R A T R A A C
O R Z E A P L R H E O B O R B L H
I A A R C O A J A C P O G L A O E
V I A D F L A U T Í N R A O J I L
E M R E C Q U A T U A L F N O V O
```

----   ------   -------   ---------

----   ------   -------   ---------

----   ------   -------   ----------

----   ------   --------   -----------

-----   ------   --------   -----------

-----   -------   ---------   ----- -- ---

-----   -------   ---------

Chapter 9

Tricky Stuff: Applications and Exceptions

Puzzle 92: Remembrance of Things Past

In this puzzle, you find encoded versions of 16 irregular past participles in Spanish. Use the verb infinitives that we provide to decode the list.

1. DNSD = OÍDO

2. PDXD

3. HTNSD

4. SNRFD

5. FTRFD

6. ZNQXD

7. UMTPXD

8. WMTQXD

9. XPLNSD

10. ZMTHXD

11. LINTPXD

12. TQRPNXD

13. NUWPTQD

14. RMINTPXD

15. PTQMTHXD

16. STQRMINTPXD

ABRIR	IMPRIMIR	ROMPER
CUBRIR	LEER	TRAER
DECIR	MORIR	VER
DESCUBRIR	~~OÍR~~	VOLVER
ESCRIBIR	PONER	
HACER	RESOLVER	

Puzzle 93: Mistaken Identity

Most students studying a foreign language encounter *false cognates* — words that resemble an English counterpart but mean something completely different. Upon hearing *embarazada* for the first time, many assume it means "embarrassed" instead of its actual meaning, "pregnant," which can be, well, embarrassing. In this puzzle, we give you an English word and its false Spanish cognate. From these two words, find the correct Spanish translation of the English word and the correct English translation of the Spanish word. For example, in the example of EMBARRASSED/EMBARAZADA, you would look for AVERGONZADO and PREGNANT.

Hint: Some of the words in this list may appear in the word search as well.

```
O D A Z N O G R E V A U G P T O L E R A T E
M A C E T O I L B I B N F N E M G R Z R R T
S E N S A T O X P U I B O T I X É N E D E K
I I W L P E D Y A N D N Ú M O C O C O P C N
D S A A S N E F R I T C U L T O I V K L I S
O S S Z G D C A I T E L A D S B C C A C P E
M E A N N T W A E A A N O Q O D A N E A E N
L C L E E O B I N A P T M C K L G J I M R S
P C I Ü O D J R T D L E I F F U L H P P E I
T U D G P L A N E Q U R R A A C O W Z A L T
N S A R X U S T I I C N N G C O O E E M A I
E H N E C K O M N E J T E T T M H A G E T V
R B F V M O O S A E N A X J O E C N N N I E
R G B V V I N D R N U U B I R T S U A T V E
U D R Z D E O F N Z T C T Ó Y R H N R O E R
C N J A V G R K E E K E E R N U G C T V P O
E A T E N F V D N R T I N S O E I I S L R T
C S N R A D U Y A S E T E E R F H O L M O S
E T L I C U E Z M D R N A P R A S W E R N K
W E L L M A N N E R E D C R E A D I N G O O
D A D I S R E V I N U R R I G N I F M O U O
D J K K O R I T S I S A O S A E M G K Y N B
```

ACTUAL/ACTUAL

ADVERTISEMENT/ADVERTENCIA

ARENA/ARENA

(TO) ASSIST/ASISTIR

(TO) ATTEND/ATENDER (2 words)

CAMP/CAMPO

COLLEGE/COLEGIO (2 words)

DISGRACE/DESGRACIA

EDUCATED/EDUCADO (hyphenated)

EMBARRASSED/EMBARAZADA

EXIT/ÉXITO

FABRIC/FÁBRICA

FAULT/FALTA

IDIOM/IDIOMA

LARGE/LARGO

LECTURE/LECTURA

LIBRARY/LIBRERÍA

(TO) PRETEND/PRETENDER

RARE (2 words)/RARO

(TO) REALIZE (3 words)/REALIZAR (2 words)

RECEIPT/RECETA

RELATIVE/RELATIVO (2 words)

SENSIBLE/SENSIBLE

SOAP/SOPA

SUCCESS/SUCESO

(TO) SUPPORT/SOPORTAR

Puzzle 94: It Takes Two

Many languages have words that can mean more than one thing, and Spanish is no exception. List two English translations for each of the 25 Spanish words, and then find both of them in the word search. For verbs, ignore the word *to* that forms the English infinitive form. Some of the translations are phrases of more than one word.

```
N T H G I R L A G E L R J M U F P N T
H O P E F O R B E G A U G N A L A N L
E T S E I R P E R E A D Y C I A S E G
S T R A I G H T A H E A D R U A H U L
K V O S E E P A K A E P H I R T E G Z
W N S U G S K L V L R F W C E G E N L
Z I I Q U N N H O E A B U H V U T O C
M O C R A T H P T W W O R R O M O T W
V S M B D C G P L X R S M A R T F B Z
U U S K N N U R O F T I A W P Z P B B
G O T E I W E A R P A B S H C T A W F
E I B H G W D Z K P R E H T A F P D C
N C S U G A R C A N E R E D T Y E A J
B I G A X F M R E T S A T E M P R Y Y
F L O O R B T A D D E B R E O R Y R W
B E A K J M M V K L L N C T Y H T O M
J D M W E D I R D E O S A Y E K N O M
M O R N I N G G C O S H L O O K A T P
B J T A G U A X N A E U E U Q T A I L
```

1. BANCO   _____   _____

2. CAÑA   _____   _____

3. COLA   _____   _____

4. DERECHO   _____   _____

5. ESPERAR   _____   _____

6. ESTACIÓN   _____   _____

7. HACER   _____   _____

8. HOJA   _____   _____

9. LENGUA   _____   _____

10. LISTO   _____   _____

11. LLEVAR   _____   _____

12. MAÑANA   _____   _____

13. MIRAR   _____   _____

14. MONO   _____   _____

15. MUÑECA   _____   _____

16. PADRE   _____   _____

17. PERDER   _____   _____

18. PICO   _____   _____

19. PISO   _____   _____

20. PROBAR   _____   _____

21. RICO   _____   _____

22. SABER   _____   _____

23. TARDE   _____   _____

24. TENER   _____   _____

25. TOMAR   _____   _____

Puzzle 95: Gender Bender

In Spanish, most words ending in *o* are masculine and most words ending in *a* are feminine, but quite a few exceptions exist. Forty-six such words appear in this grid; 36 are masculine words ending in *a* and the remaining 10 are feminine words ending in *o*. Can you find them all?

```
M E A M A R G O R P A O L L A M E T
A M A R G I C U R C M M E M R R I Á
M O R F E M A A Í V A U E O T O F P
O R O P L A N E T A R N O T H O E O
T G E A I O N A R P O S L O S A O A
N Y I R U J B Í A F N X E L A I C M
Í A A T T R A N V Í A E D I P A S O
S A M Í S R O M S A P Ó O P A T I L
O L G E D E O N A M T D M M M A D P
A I É G U E T A U R A M O R A R F I
T R D D A Q U A A E G U A R D I A D
E O U A B M S O M M N A N H S P N A
O G A C R I S E R E E I I C E C T D
P A M I L C H I O D L L G D R O A M
A P O L I C Í A R R C B I M I A S O
L O I G A R E O R A M A O D A O M T
I N D Í G E N A M M C U I R A Z A O
B E I T E L E G R A M A A P P R E O
```

Puzzle 96: What the El?

The following English words have something in common: they're feminine in Spanish but take the masculine article *el* in the singular form. Convert them into Spanish, and then insert the Spanish equivalents into the blanks to form sentences in English; the inserted words may span more than one word. Note that the last sentence contains two blanks.

1. Mary ___HAD A___ little lamb.

2. Ana thanked the host for _____RY nice evening.

3. Violeta Chamorro was the first female president of NICAR_____.

4. José bought a large-screen PL_____ television for the den.

5. JE_____UDE Van Damme starred in the movie "Double Impact."

6. CAB_____ND Acan were two Mayan gods.

7. The meat sandwich was made with _____AD, and mustard.

8. The bank teller asked me to sign the check WIT_____CK pen.

9. We danced the rumba, tango, and C_____ at the dance marathon.

10. "We can't go to Cuba and not visit the capital, La _____NA," said Olga to the travel agent.

11. "Have you seen any of the plays by Honoré de B_____C?"

12. The plane spent 30 minutes on the T_____C after taxiing.

13. Rosa's favorite song was "Diamonds _____ Girl's Best Friend."

14. "That comedy movie was so funny; it was a RE_____S!"

15. Miguel aptly named his new d_____TIAN "Spot."

16. Francisco's favorite judge on "American Idol" was P_____ Abdul.

17. Rita forgot to buy _____RAGUS from the greengrocer.

18. The student's short attention span made him very DISTR_____BLE.

19. Abuelita used to enjoy watching Ricardo MONT_____N on "Fantasy Island."

20. Héctor walked along the EMB_____DERO when he visited San Francisco.

21. Pedro didn't want the dinner special, so he ordered from the _____C_____ menu.

ACT   _____

ANCHOR   _____

AREA   _____

ART   _____

ASTHMA   _____

AXE   _____

BEAN   _____

BIRD   _____

CHEST/BOX   _____

CLASSROOM   _____

CROSS   _____

DAWN   _____

EAGLE   _____

~~FAIRY~~   _____HADA_____

HUNGER   _____

INCREASE/RISE   _____

SEAWEED   _____

SOUL   _____

SPEECH (MANNER OF SPEAKING)   _____

WATER   _____

WEAPON   _____

WING   _____

Puzzle 97: Searching for Meaning

The following 20 Spanish words have an unusual property — they take different meanings depending on whether they use the masculine article *el* or the feminine article *la*. English definitions of the two meanings for each of the 20 words are hidden in the word search below. Can you find all 40 words and phrases in the grid?

Hint: Several of the words you're looking for in the grid are direct cognates; it's up to you to determine which ones they are.

```
R A T P Q E U D N A M M O C O L E C H
K A M O C D I S C O T H E Q U E J L L
N O I S S I M S N A R T L A N G I S P
A R H A B Z W E B R L I C D U W H A O
B O S N A D Y K E R X H Y I E N I P L
R N I G T E G D E N A T D R A A L U I
E C F E U F I D S M I E N E R M L B C
V E V R F T R E P C P N O C R E S L E
I D C R O O R I L R I G I T I C I I F
R O O R Y U O A P G N T T O N I D S O
T N I L C N T T R U O C R R G L E H R
T A O U S I C A L A I D O Y P O P E C
L H T H P P M T S E I R P J P P G R E
U M I A O M H A R E L O H C N A G E R
Q P C T O F F S K E J C X U S F G R O
W D A C K W A K I S T E F S I F Y E Y
R T T R A N S I S T O R E N D J Z X R
O U Q D A E H E R O F M B E N D I N G
S E A R C H E N E L O N O I T A T S N
```

BUSCA

CAPITAL

CÓLERA

COMA

CORTE

CURA

DISCO

EDITORIAL

FINAL

FRENTE

GUÍA

MARGEN

ORDEN

PAPA

PARTE

PENDIENTE

PEZ

POLICÍA

RADIO

TERMINAL

Puzzle 98: The Sixteen Commandments

Eight Spanish verbs are irregular when used as commands in the second-person singular. They appear in the grid below in their positive and negative forms. Can you find all sixteen commands and deduce their infinitives?

```
T A P O S V E L T I G
O N S Z Í A S A L O N
N O R A N A E S Z A H
G O S I G O O S O Y N
I D T A C L V F O R E
C B H E G O A A Z N V
É O N T N I N S Y S É
N X É U E G D E O A I
D D A Á T F A O P N S
N O P O N G A S N O L
S A G N E V O N R O N
```

--   ---   -- ------

--   ---   -- ------

--   -- ----   -- ------

---   -- -----   -- ------

---   -- -----

---   -- -----

Puzzle 99: Looking to the Future

Unscramble the following English words and phrases to form an irregular future tense form in Spanish. The conjugations appear in parentheses as a hint, and a list of the infinitives follows. Most of the Spanish future tenses contain accent marks.

1. HEAR (first person, singular)   _____

2. NADIR (third person, plural)   _____

3. REHAB (first person, singular)   _____

4. ALDERS (first person, singular)   _____

5. ARDENT (third person, singular)   _____

6. DENVER (first person, singular)   _____

7. LAVARD (third person, singular)   _____

8. PARDON (third person, singular)   _____

9. PARDON (third person, plural)   _____

10. SCARAB (second person, singular) _____

CABER	PODER	VALER
DECIR	PONER	VENIR
HABER	SALIR	
HACER	TENER	

Puzzle 100: Past Masters

All the clues in this crossword are from the past — particularly the 16 verbs in Spanish that have irregular preterite forms. Given a conjugation, fill in the verb infinitive in the grid. Two verbs have the exact same conjugations, but their infinitives have different lengths.

Across

3 SUPO

4 HUBISTE

6 TRAJE

8 DIJIMOS

10 PUDIERON

11 TUVE

12 QUISE

Down

1 VINO

2 CUPIMOS

3 FUI

4 HIZO

5 FUIMOS

7 ANDUVIERON

8 DI

9 ESTUVO

10 PUSISTE

Puzzle 101: Work Conditions

Unscramble the English words and phrases below to form a conjugation of an irregular conditional form for one of the ten irregular verbs. In addition to the verb, we tell you whether the form you want is first, second, or third person, and singular or plural.

1. RADII (first or third person, singular) _____

2. CARIBA (first or third person, singular) _____

3. SHARIA (second person, singular) _____

4. BAHRAIN (third person, plural) _____

5. PONIARD (third person, plural) _____

6. PONIARD (first or third person, singular) _____

7. RADIALS (first or third person, singular) _____

8. VIRAL AD (first or third person, singular) _____

9. INVADERS (second person, singular) _____

10. STRAINED (second person, singular) _____

CABER	PODER	VALER
DECIR	PONER	VENIR
HABER	SALIR	
HACER	TENER	

Puzzle 102: Location, Location

If you travel throughout the Spanish-speaking world, you may notice that different regions and countries may use different words to mean the same thing. This discrepancy is particularly common in words used in Spain versus Latin America.

The 15 numbered English words have two Spanish translations — one of them common in Spain and the other in Latin America. After you match them all, enter the Spanish words in the two grids so that one grid contains all of the Castilian words (used in Spain) and the other contains their Latin American counterparts. Both solutions are unique.

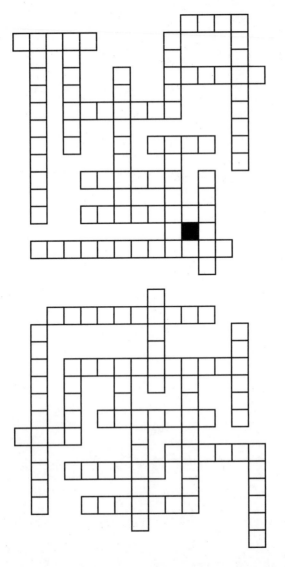

	Castilian	*Latin American*
1. DRIVER	CHÓFER	CHOFER
2. APRICOT		
3. BUS		
4. CAR		
5. COMPUTER		
6. DRIVE (VERB)		
7. EYEGLASSES		
8. FRUIT JUICE		
9. GREEN BEANS		
10. OKAY		
11. PARK (VERB)		
12. PEACH		
13. POTATO		
14. PULLOVER		
15. TICKET		

ALBARICOQUE	CONDUCIR	JUGO
APARCAR	DAMASCO	LENTES
AUTOBÚS	DE ACUERDO	MANEJAR
BILLETE	DURAZNO	MELOCOTÓN
BOLETO	ESTACIONAR	ORDENADOR
CARRO	GAFAS	PAPA
~~CHOFER~~	GUAGUA	PATATA
~~CHÓFER~~	HABICHUELAS	SUÉTER
COCHE	JERSEY	VALE
COMPUTADORA	JUDÍAS VERDES	ZUMO

Puzzle 103: Wikipuzzle

The letters K and W are relatively uncommon in Spanish, except for words borrowed from other languages. You discover some of these rare examples by cracking the cryptogram. Because most of the words are cognates, we provide brief descriptions rather than direct translations as hints below. Except for the first example, all of the words in this list are in alphabetical order.

1. SJRJ = KIWI
2. STBHJYFIOFZJF
3. STETQH
4. STEQJWK
5. STXTO
6. SHWJT
7. SJBF
8. SJUFWF
9. SJWYHEKTEQHW
10. SJWHIJFBFKJT
11. SJFISF
12. SFIGHE
13. SEJZQFW

14. SVRTJQ
15. RTCBHEF
16. RTBSJEJT
17. RTZJQJ
18. RTQHE
19. RTQHEZFBF
20. RHM
21. RHMOTU
22. RHBQHE
23. RGJISX
24. RJWYIVECJWK
25. RJWYIVECJIQT
26. RFBCETUJF

ACCORDING TO JEWISH DIETARY LAW

AFRICAN COUNTRY

ALCOHOLIC BEVERAGE

AQUATIC SPORT WITH A BALL AND NET

BOXER'S WEIGHT CLASS

CAMERA USED FOR TRANSMITTING INTERNET IMAGES

CANOE USED BY ESKIMOS

ELK

~~FRUIT WITH FUZZY SKIN~~

GO-CART RACING

INERT GAS

INSTRUMENT WITH COLORED MATERIAL AND MIRRORS

JAPANESE ROBE-LIKE GARMENT

MARTIAL ART

METRIC PREFIX MEANING "THOUSAND"

NEWSSTAND

PART OF THE INTERNET

PERSIAN GULF NATION

SAILBOARDER

SAILBOARDING

SCHOOL BEFORE FIRST GRADE

SLANG FOR LAVATORY OR WASHROOM

STUDY OF MECHANICS OF HUMAN MOVEMENT

TUNGSTEN, DERIVED FROM ITS GERMAN NAME

VALKYRIE

WAFFLE IRON

Part III
The Solutions

The 5th Wave   By Rich Tennant

"I'm looking for a Spanish word games book that focuses on smooth introductions, alluring conversation, irresistibly charming phrases, that sort of thing."

In this part...

We're not going to be the Spanish Inquisition in puzzle form here and leave you wondering what you did wrong. Part of the fun of puzzle-solving is checking to see how well you did and to get the satisfaction of a job well done. You also need to be able to check your work, correct any mistakes, and beef up your understanding through translations. We don't want to leave you dissatisfied (or cursing our names), so here they are. All we ask is that you not open up this section before you've given a puzzle your best effort.

Chapter 10

Solutions

Puzzle 1

1. HOLA. ¿CÓMO ESTÁS?
2. MUY BIEN, GRACIAS. ¿Y TÚ?
3. BASTANTE BIEN, GRACIAS.
4. SOY DIEGO. ¿CÓMO TE LLAMAS?
5. ME LLAMO SUSANA.
6. ENCANTADO, SUSANA.
7. MUCHO GUSTO, DIEGO.
8. ¿DE DÓNDE ERES, SUSANA?
9. SOY DE NUEVA YORK. ¿Y TÚ?
10. SOY DE CALIFORNIA.
11. ¿ADÓNDE VAS AHORA?
12. VOY AL CINE. ¿Y TÚ?
13. VOY AL MERCADO.
14. BUENO, ¡NOS VEMOS PRONTO!
15. PUES, ¡HASTA LUEGO, DIEGO!
16. ADIÓS, SUSANA.

Puzzle 2

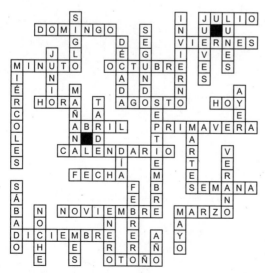

Puzzle 3

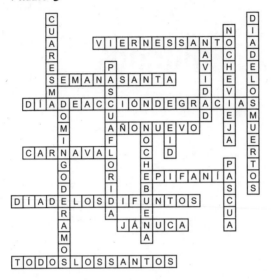

Puzzle 4

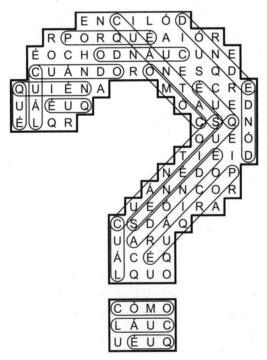

1. QUÉ (WHAT TIME IS IT?)
2. CÓMO (WHAT IS YOUR NAME?)
3. QUIÉN (WHO KNOWS?)
4. CUÁNTOS (HOW OLD ARE YOU?)
5. CUÁL (WHAT IS TODAY'S DATE?)
6. CUÁNDO (WHEN IS YOUR BIRTHDAY?)
7. POR QUÉ (WHY DO YOU STUDY SPANISH?)
8. QUÉ (WHAT'S NEW?)
9. DÓNDE (WHERE IS THE BATHROOM?)
10. CUÁL (WHAT IS YOUR TELEPHONE NUMBER?)
11. DÓNDE (WHERE ARE YOU FROM?)
12. CÓMO (HOW ARE YOU?)
13. QUÉ (WHAT DOES IT MEAN?)
14. QUIÉNES (WHO ARE YOUR FRIENDS?)
15. QUÉ (WHAT'S THE WEATHER TODAY?)
16. CUÁNTAS (HOW MANY GIRLS ARE IN THE FAMILY?)
17. POR QUÉ (WHY DON'T YOU HAVE THE MONEY?)
18. CUÁL (WHAT IS THE CAPITAL OF COLOMBIA?)
19. ADÓNDE ([TO] WHERE ARE YOU GOING ON MONDAY?)
20. CUÁNDO (WHEN DO YOU GRADUATE FROM COLLEGE?)

Puzzle 5

1. NEGRO (black)
2. AMARILLO (yellow)
3. ANARANJADO (orange)
4. MARRÓN (brown)
5. ROJO (red)
6. BLANCO (white)
7. VERDE (green)
8. BRONCEADO (bronze)
9. AZUL (blue)
10. ROSADO (pink)
11. BLANCUZCO (off-white)
12. GRIS (gray)
13. MORADO (purple)
14. DORADO (gold)
15. LAVANDA (lavender)

Puzzle 6

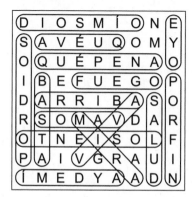

The hidden phrase is "¡NO ME DIGA!" which means "YOU DON'T SAY!"

Puzzle 7

DOS (2)	SEIS (6)	CATORCE (14)
MIL (1,000)	TRECE (13)	CUARENTA (40)
UNO (1)	NUEVE (9)	CINCUENTA (50)
CIEN (100)	CINCO (5)	DIECISÉIS (16)
TRES (3)	SIETE (7)	DIECIOCHO (18)
DOCE (12)	QUINCE (15)	DIECINUEVE (19)
ONCE (11)	CUATRO (4)	DIECISIETE (17)
DIEZ (10)	VEINTE (20)	SESENTA Y DOS (62)
OCHO (8)	TREINTA (30)	

The sum is 1492 — the year of Christopher Columbus's voyage to the Americas.

Puzzle 8

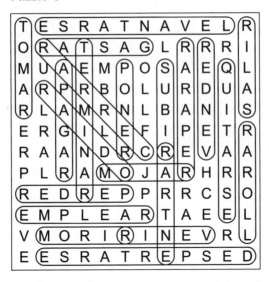

The verb infinitives in the grid (followed by their translations and then their counterparts in the word list) are: APAGAR (turn off, ENCENDER), CERRAR (close, ABRIR), DESPERTARSE (wake up, ACOSTARSE), EMPLEAR (hire, DESPEDIR), ENTRAR (enter, SALIR), GASTAR (spend, AHORRAR), LEVANTARSE (stand up, SENTARSE), LLORAR (cry, REÍR), MOJAR (dampen, SECAR), MORIR (die, VIVIR), ODIAR (hate, AMAR), PERDER (lose, ENCONTRAR), PONER (put in, SACAR), QUITARSE (take off clothing, PONERSE), REPARAR (repair, ROMPER), SALIR (leave, LLEGAR), SUBIR (go up, BAJAR), TERMINAR (end, finish, COMENZAR, EMPEZAR), TOMAR (take, DAR), VENDER (sell, COMPRAR), and VENIR (come, IR).

Puzzle 9

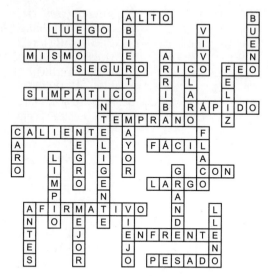

Puzzle 10

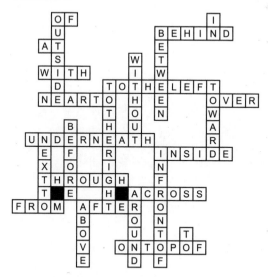

Puzzle 11

1. IR (go)
2. DAR (give)
3. OÍR (hear)
4. VER (see)
5. LEER (read)
6. ABRIR (open)
7. BEBER (drink)
8. CABER (fit)
9. COMER (eat)
10. CREER (think)

11. DECIR (say, tell)
12. HACER (do, make
13. JUGAR (play [a game])
14. MIRAR (look)
15. PAGAR (pay)
16. PODER (be able)
17. PONER (put)
18. SABER (know [facts], know how)
19. SALIR (leave)
20. TENER (have)
21. TOMAR (take)
22. TRAER (bring)
23. VIVIR (live)
24. CERRAR (close)
25. CONTAR (tell, relate)
26. DESEAR (want, desire)
27. DORMIR (sleep)
28. HABLAR (speak)
29. PENSAR (think)
30. PERDER (lose)
31. VENDER (sell)

32. VIAJAR (travel)
33. CAMBIAR (change, exchange)
34. COMPRAR (buy)
35. CONOCER (know [be acquainted with])
36. LIMPIAR (clean)
37. APRENDER (learn)
38. COMENZAR (begin, start)
39. ESCRIBIR (write)
40. ESCUCHAR (listen)
41. ESTUDIAR (study)
42. INTENTAR (try, intend)
43. PERMITIR (allow)
44. TERMINAR (end)
45. UTILIZAR (use)
46. ENCONTRAR (find)
47. NECESITAR (need)
48. PREGUNTAR (ask)
49. RESPONDER (answer)
50. COMPRENDER (understand, comprehend)

Puzzle 12

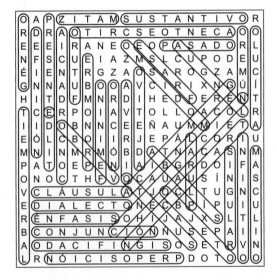

The words in the grid in alphabetical order are: ACENTO ESCRITO (accent mark), ADJETIVO (adjective), ADVERBIO (adverb), ARTÍCULO (article), CLÁUSULA (clause), CONCORDANCIA (agreement), CONJUGACIÓN (conjugation), CONJUNCIÓN (conjunction), DEFINICIÓN (definition), DIALECTO (dialect), ÉNFASIS (stress), FEMININO (feminine), FRASE (phrase), FUTURO (future), GÉNERO (gender), GRAMÁTICA (grammar), INFINITIVO (infinitive), LENGUA (language), MASCULINO (masculine), MATIZ (meaning [nuance]), MODISMO (idiom), NÚMERO (number), OBJETO (object), ORACIÓN (sentence), PASADO (past [tense]), PLURAL (plural), PREPOSICIÓN (preposition), PRESENTE (present [tense]), PRONOMBRE (pronoun), SIGNIFICADO (meaning), SÍLABA (syllable), SINGULAR (singular), SUJETO (subject), SUSTANTIVO (noun), TIEMPO VERBAL (verb tense), TILDE (tilde), TRADUCCIÓN (translation), and VERBO (verb).

Puzzle 13

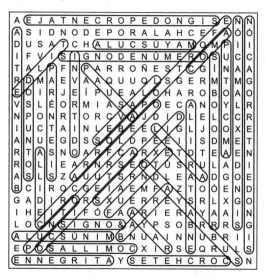

The words in the grid are: APÓSTROFE (apostrophe), ARROBA (at sign), ASTERISCO (asterisk), BARRA (slash), BARRA INVERTIDA (backslash), CEDILLA (cedilla), CIRCUNFLEJO (circumflex), COMA (comma), COMILLAS (quotation marks), CORCHETES (brackets), DIÉRESIS (dieresis), DOS PUNTOS (colon), EN BASTARDILLA (italics), EN NEGRITA (boldface), FUENTE (font), INVERTIDO (upside-down), LETRA (letter), LLAVES (braces), MAYÚSCULA (uppercase), MINÚSCULA (lowercase), PARÉNTESIS (parenthesis), PAUSA (pause), PUNTO (period), PUNTO Y COMA (semicolon), RAYA (dash), SIGNO & (ampersand, pronounced "el signo Y," as in the Spanish word for "and"), SIGNO DE EXCLAMACIÓN (exclamation point), SIGNO DE INTERROGACIÓN (question mark), SIGNO DE NÚMERO (number sign), SIGNO DE PORCENTAJE (percentage sign), SIGNO DEL DÓLAR (dollar sign), SUBRAYADO (underlined), and TILDE (tilde).

Puzzle 14

1. AMADO (loved)
2. FELIZ (happy)
3. LISTO (ready
4. ALEGRE (glad)
5. CELOSO (jealous)
6. CÓMODO (comfortable)
7. TRISTE (sad)
8. ANIMADO (excited)
9. CANSADO (tired)
10. ENOJADO (angry)
11. EXTRAÑO (strange)
12. MIEDOSO (afraid)
13. QUERIDO (beloved)
14. ABURRIDO (bored)
15. ASUSTADO (scared)
16. CONTENTO (pleased)
17. INCÓMODO (uncomfortable)

18. NERVIOSO (nervous)
19. ASOMBRADO (stunned)
20. ENVIDIOSO (envious)
21. TRANQUILO (calm)
22. AFORTUNADO (fortunate/
    lucky)
23. AGRADECIDO (thankful)
24. CONFUNDIDO (confused)
25. DESPISTADO (absent-minded)
26. PREOCUPADO (worried)
27. SOSPECHOSO (suspicious)
28. AVERGONZADO (ashamed/
    embarrassed)
29. SORPRENDIDO (surprised)
30. DESILUSIONADO
    (disappointed/disillusioned)

Puzzle 15

Puzzle 16

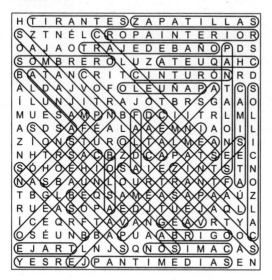

The 40 hidden articles of clothing are: ABRIGO (coat), BLUSA (blouse), BOLSA (purse), BOTAS (boots), BRAGA (panties), BUFANDA (scarf), CALCETINES (socks), CALZONCILLOS (briefs), CALZONES (long johns), CAMISA (shirt), CAMISETA (T-shirt), CAMISÓN (nightgown), CHALECO (vest), CHAQUETA (jacket), CINTURÓN (belt), CORBATA (tie), DELANTAL (apron), FAJA (girdle), FALDA (skirt), GUANTES (gloves), IMPERMEABLE (raincoat), JERSEY (pullover), MANTÓN (shawl), PAJARITA (bow tie), PANTALONES (pants), MEDIAS (pantyhose), PAÑUELO (handkerchief), PIJAMAS (pajamas), ROPA INTERIOR (underwear), SANDALIAS (sandals), SOMBRERO (hat), SOSTÉN (brassiere), SUÉTER (sweater), TIRANTES (suspenders), TRAJE (suit), TRAJE DE BAÑO (bathing suit), VAQUEROS (jeans), VESTIDO (dress), ZAPATILLAS (slippers), and ZAPATOS (shoes).

Puzzle 17

1. HACER LA CAMA
2. SACUDIR LOS MUEBLES
3. PLANCHAR LA ROPA
4. COCINAR UN PASTEL
5. CORTAR EL CÉSPED
6. PAGAR LAS CUENTAS
7. PLANEAR UNA FIESTA

8. SACAR LA BASURA
9. RECICLAR LOS PERIÓDICOS
10. BARRER EL SUELO
11. LAVAR LOS PLATOS
12. PODAR LAS PLANTAS
13. PINTAR EL GARAJE
14. CERAR EL COCHE

Puzzle 18

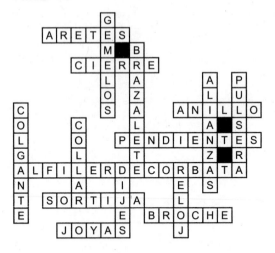

Puzzle 19

Puzzle 20

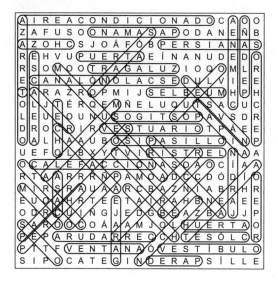

The entries in this word search are: AIRE ACONDICIONADO (air conditioning), BALCÓN (balcony), BANCO (bench), CABAÑA (cabin), CALEFACCIÓN (heating system), CANALÓN (gutter), CASA (house), CERRADURA (lock), CHIMENEA (fireplace), CHOZA (hut), CLÓSET (walk-in closet), CUARTO (room), DESVÁN (attic/loft), ESCALERA (stairway), ESCALÓN (step), GARAJE (garage), HOGAR (home/hearth), HUERTA (kitchen garden), JARDÍN (garden), MARQUESINA (canopy), MUEBLES (furniture), MURALLA (security wall), MURO (garden wall), PARARRAYOS (lightning rod), PARED (wall), PASAMANO (handrail), PASILLO (hallway), PATIO (patio), PELDAÑO (stairstep), PERCHA (coat hanger), PERCHERO (coat rack), PERSIANAS (venetian blinds), PISCINA (swimming pool), PISO (floor [story]), POSTIGOS (shutters), PUERTA (door/gate), RADIADOR (radiator), REJA (iron grille [window]), RISTREL (molding), ROPERO (closet), SETO (hedge), SÓTANO (basement), SUELO (floor [walkable surface]), TAPIA (retaining wall), TECHO (roof), TERRAZA (terrace), TIMBRE (doorbell), TOLDO (awning), TRAGALUZ (cellar window), TUBERÍA (plumbing), VENTANA (window), VESTÍBULO (entryway), and VESTUARIO (cloakroom).

Puzzle 21

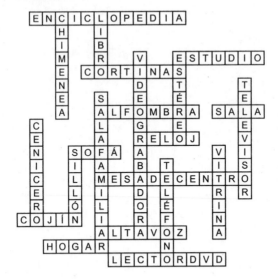

Puzzle 22

1. DISCO (record)
2. RADIO (radio transmitter)
3. ANTENA (antenna)
4. CASETE (cassette)
5. ESCÁNER (scanner)
6. ESTÉREO (stereo)
7. ALTAVOCES (speakers)
8. AUDÍFONOS (headphones)
9. AURICULAR (earpiece/headset)
10. COPIADORA (copy machine)
11. PAGINADOR (pager)
12. BANDA ANCHA (broadband)
13. LECTOR DE CD (CD player)
14. VIDEOCÁMARA (camcorder/video camera)
15. CONTROL REMOTO (remote control)
16. CÁMARA DIGITAL (digital camera)
17. DISCO COMPACTO (compact disc)
18. TELÉFONO CELULAR (cell/mobile phone)
19. ALARMA ANTIRROBO (burglar alarm)
20. INTERCOMUNICADOR (intercom)
21. REPRODUCTOR DE DVD (DVD player)
22. TRITURADORA DE PAPEL (paper shredder)
23. COMPUTADORA PORTÁTIL (laptop/notebook computer)
24. SISTEMA DE CINE EN CASA (home theater system)
25. COMPUTADORA DE ESCRITORIO (desktop computer)
26. TELEVISOR DE PANTALLA ANCHA (wide-screen television)
27. TELEVISOR DE PANTALLA PLANA (flat-screen television)

Puzzle 23

1. CUNA (cradle)
2. BELÉN (crib)
3. MÓVIL (mobile)
4. MANTA (blanket)
5. TALCO (baby powder)
6. LITERA (bunk bed)
7. MOISÉS (bassinet)
8. PAÑALES (diapers)
9. SONAJERO (rattle)
10. CAMBIADOR (changing table)
11. LAMPARILLA (night light)
12. SILLA ALTA (high chair)
13. BALDAQUÍN (bed canopy)
14. OSO DE PELUCHE (teddy bear)
15. CAJA DE MÚSICA (music box)
16. SILLITA DE PASEO (stroller)
17. JUGUETE DE TRAPO (stuffed toy)
18. COCHECITO DE BEBÉ (baby carriage)
19. PORTAPAÑALES (diaper bag)
20. TOALLITAS HÚMEDAS (baby wipes)
21. CABALLITO MECEDOR (rocking horse)
22. HABITACIÓN DE LOS NIÑOS (nursery)

Puzzle 24

Puzzle 25

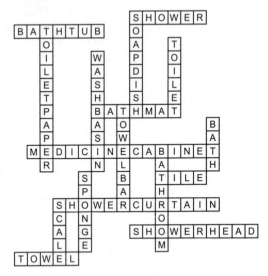

Puzzle 26

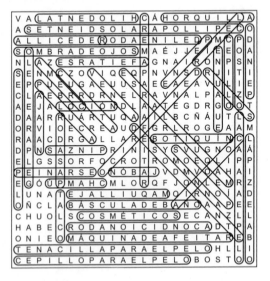

Puzzle 27

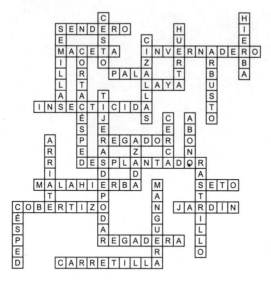

Puzzle 28

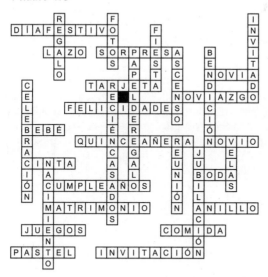

Puzzle 29

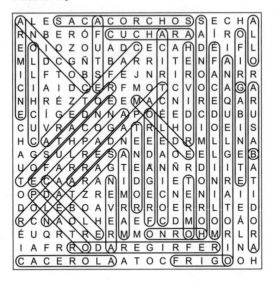

The 34 kitchen items are: AGARRADOR (pot holder), ANAQUEL GIRATORIO (revolving shelf), BASURA (garbage), BATIDORA (mixer), CABLE (electric cord), CACEROLA (saucepan), CAFETERA (coffeepot), COCINA (kitchen), COCINA ELÉCTRICA (electric cooker), CUCHARA (spoon), CUCHILLO (knife), ENCHUFE (plug), ENCIMERA (counter), ESTUFA (stove), FREGADERO (sink), FRIGO (fridge), GABINETE (cupboard), GRIFO (faucet), HERVIDOR (kettle), HORNO (oven), HORNO DE MICROONDAS (microwave oven), MARMITA (casserole dish), MOLDE (baking tin), MOLINILLO DE CAFÉ (coffee grinder), NEVERA (freezer), OLLA (pot), PLATO (dish), REFRIGERADOR (refrigerator), SACACORCHOS (corkscrew), SARTÉN (frying pan), TAPADERA (lid), TENEDOR (fork), TERMO (thermos), and TOSTADOR (toaster).

Puzzle 30

1. LAS MANZANAS
   (the apples)
2. LAS PERAS
   (the pears)
3. LAS NARANJAS
   (the oranges)
4. LOS LIMONES
   (the lemons)
5. LAS TORONJAS
   (the grapefruits)
6. LOS PLÁTANOS
   (the bananas)
7. LAS CEREZAS
   (the cherries)
8. LAS CALABAZAS
   (the pumpkins)
9. LAS FRAMBUESAS
   (the raspberries)
10. LAS FRESAS
    (the strawberries)
11. LOS DURAZNOS
    (the peaches)
12. LAS SANDÍAS
    (the watermelons)

Puzzle 31

1. NABO (turnip), APIO (celery)
2. PAPA (potato), MAÍZ (corn)
3. PEPINO (cucumber), RÁBANO (radish)
4. CEBOLLA (onion), LECHUGA (lettuce)
5. COLINABO (rutabaga), COLIFLOR (cauliflower)
6. GUISANTE (pea), PIMIENTO (pepper)
7. REMOLACHA (beet), BERENJENA (eggplant)
8. ZANAHORIA (carrot), ESPINACAS (spinach)
9. ALCACHOFA (artichoke), ESPÁRRAGO (asparagus)

Puzzle 32

1. CARNE
2. PAVO
3. POLLO
4. PUERCO
5. BISTEC
6. CORDERO
7. TERNERO
8. CHULETA
9. COSTILLA
10. CARNE DE RES

Puzzle 33

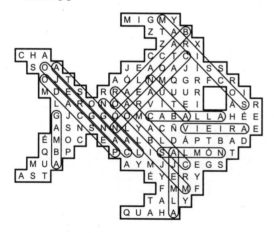

The fourteen words found in the puzzle are: ALMEJA (clam), ATÚN (tuna), BACALAO (cod), CABALLA (mackerel), CALAMAR (squid), CAMARÓN (shrimp), CANGREJO (crab), GAMBA (prawn), LANGOSTA (lobster), MARISCOS (shellfish/seafood), MEJILLÓN (mussel), PESCADO (fish), SALMÓN (salmon), and VIEIRA (scallop).

Puzzle 34

1. TÉ (tea)
2. CAFÉ (coffee)
3. AGUA (water)
4. VINO (wine)
5. JUGO (juice)
6. SIDRA (cider)
7. LECHE (milk)
8. COÑAC (brandy/cognac)
9. TOMAR (to drink)
10. BEBER (to drink)
11. COCTEL (cocktail)
12. BEBIDA (drink)
13. GASEOSA (soda/carbonated drink)
14. CERVEZA (beer)
15. LIMONADA (lemonade)
16. CHAMPAÑA (champagne)
17. REFRESCO (soft drink)
18. AGUA MINERAL (mineral water)
19. AGUA EMBOTELLADA (bottled water)
20. CAVA
21. SANGRÍA
22. TEQUILA
23. HORCHATA
24. CALIMOCHO
25. VINO DE JEREZ
26. TINTO DE VERANO

Puzzle 35

1. LOS POSTRES (desserts)
2. EL FLAN (custard)
3. LA FRUTA (fruit)
4. LA TORTA (pie)
5. EL QUESO (cheese)
6. LA CANELA (cinnamon)
7. EL PASTEL (cake/pastry)
8. EL HELADO (ice cream)
9. LOS DULCES (candy/sweets)
10. LA GALLETA (cookie)
11. EL MAZAPÁN (marzipan)
12. EL SORBETE (sorbet)
13. LOS DÁTILES (dates)
14. LA GELATINA (gelatin)
15. EL CARAMELO (hard candy)
16. EL CHOCOLATE (chocolate)
17. EL DULCE DE LECHE (caramel sauce)
18. EL ARROZ CON LECHE (rice pudding)
19. LAS YEMAS
20. EL TURRÓN
21. LOS CHURROS
22. EL TEMBLEQUE
23. LOS POLVORONES
24. LA ROSCA DE REYES
25. LAS CALAVERAS DE AZÚCAR

Puzzle 36

1. LA LOCIÓN
2. LA MEDICINA
3. EL BÁLSAMO
4. LA PASTILLA
5. LA CÁPSULA
6. LA PÍLDORA
7. LAS ASPIRINAS
8. EL PARCHE
9. EL UNGÜENTO
10. EL ANTIDOTO
11. EL INHALADOR
12. EL ANTIBIÓTICO
13. EL ANTIHISTAMÍNICO
14. LOS MEDICAMENTOS
15. LA PASTILLA PARA LA TOS
16. EL DECONGESTIONANTE

Puzzle 37

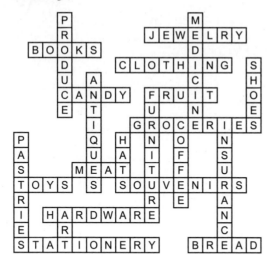

Puzzle 38

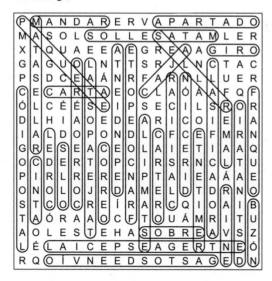

The words in the grid are: APARTADO (post office box), BUZÓN (mailbox), CAJA (box), CARTA (letter), CARTERO (letter carrier [masc.]), CINTA (tape), CLASIFICADORA (sorting machine), CLASIFICAR (sort [verb]), CÓDIGO POSTAL (zip/postal code), CORDEL (string), CORREO (post office), CORREO AÉREO (air mail), DEPENDIENTA (clerk [fem.]), DESTINATARIO (addressee), DIRECCIÓN (address), ENTREGA ESPECIAL (special delivery), ENVIAR (send), ESTAMPILLA (stamp), FRANCO DE PORTE (free shipping), FRANQUEO (postage), GASTOS DE ENVÍO (postage and handling), GIRO (money order), LAMER (lick [verb]), MANDAR (send), MATASELLAR (cancel/postmark [verb]), MATASELLOS (postmark [noun]), PAQUETE (package), REMITENTE (sender), SELLAR (seal [verb]), SELLO (stamp), SOBRE (envelope), and TARJETA POSTAL (postcard).

Puzzle 39

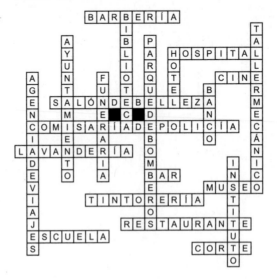

Puzzle 40

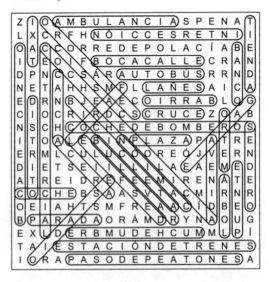

The 36 words in alphabetical order are: ACERA (sidewalk), AMBULANCIA (ambulance), ÁRBOL (tree), AUTOBÚS (bus),

AVENIDA (avenue), BANCO (bank/bench), BARRIO (neighbor-
hood), BICICLETA (bicycle), BOCACALLE (side street/street entry),
BOCA DE INCENDIO (fire hydrant), BULEVAR (boulevard), CAMIÓN
(truck), CANCHA (sports field), CENTRO COMERCIAL (shopping
mall), COCHE (car), COCHE DE BOMBEROS (fire engine), COCHE
DE POLICÍA (police car), CRUCE (crossing), DESFILE (parade),
DISTRITO (district), ESTACIÓN DE TRENES (train station), ESTADIO
(stadium), FAROL (street light), GARAJE (garage), INTERSECCIÓN
(intersection), METRO (subway), MUCHEDUMBRE (crowd), PARADA
(stop), PASO DE PEATONES (pedestrian crossing), PLAZA (plaza/
square), PUENTE (bridge), SEMÁFORO (traffic light), SEÑAL (sign),
SENDERO (path), TAXI (taxi), and TIENDA (store).

Puzzle 41

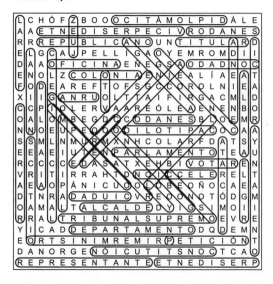

The 50 words in the grid are: AGENCIA (agency), ALCALDE (mayor),
ASAMBLEA (assembly), AYUNTAMIENTO (city council, city hall),
CANDIDATO (candidate), CAPITOLIO (capitol), CENSO (census),
CIUDAD (city), COLEGIO ELECTORAL (polling place, electoral
college), COLONIA (colony), CONDADO (county), CONGRESO
(congress), CONSERVADOR (conservative), CONSTITUCIÓN (consti-
tution), CORTE (court), DEMOCRACIA (democracy), DEMÓCRATA
(Democrat), DEPARTAMENTO (bureau, department), DICTADOR
(dictator), DIPLOMACIA (diplomacy), DIPLOMÁTICO (diplomat),
ELECCIÓN (election), ELEGIR (to elect), ENMIENDA (amendment),
ESTADO (state), FEDERAL (federal), GOBERNADOR (governor),
GOBIERNO (government), IMPUESTO (tax), JUEZ (judge), LEY (law),
LIBERAL (liberal), MUNICIPAL (municipal), NACIONAL (national),
OFICINA (office), PARLAMENTO (parliament), PETICIÓN (petition),
PRESIDENTE (president), PRIMER MINISTRO (prime minister),

REPRESENTANTE (representative), REPUBLICANO (Republican), SECRETARIO (secretary), SENADO (senate), SENADOR (senator), TITULAR (officeholder), TRIBUNAL SUPREMO (supreme court), URNA (ballot box), VICEPRESIDENTE (vice president), VOTAR (vote [verb]), and VOTO (vote [noun]).

Puzzle 42

```
                    I N T E R É S
            B               A                   G
            A   C A M B I A R                   I
            N   U           J                   R
        C H E Q U E   E N E F E C T I V O       O
            U ■ N           T                   P
    E       V E N T A N I L L A   P A G O       O
    N       R A               D               S
    D       O   D E V O L V E R               T
C O B R A R       E           C               A
    S   H   P A G A R   B     R   G           L
B A N C O   R       H   I     É   A
    R   R É         O   L     D I N E R O
        P R E S T A R   L     I ■ A
        A ■ T       R   E     T A R I F A
C A J E R O A U T O M Á T I C O
            M       S     E   A
            O             A   M O N E D A
                          B
        C U E N T A C O R R I E N T E
                          O
```

Puzzle 43

1. SAL (salt)
2. CAFÉ (café)
3. COPA (goblet)
4. MESA (table)
5. MENÚ (menu [offerings])
6. SOPA (soup)
7. VASO (glass)
8. BARRA (counter)
9. CARTA (menu [printed])
10. CRUDO (raw)
11. PLATO (plate)
12. SILLA (chair)
13. ACEITE (oil)
14. A PUNTO (medium)
15. BEBIDA (beverage, drink)
16. COMIDA (meal)
17. CUENTA (bill, check)
18. MESERA (waitress)
19. MESERO (waiter)
20. POSTRE (dessert)
21. CAPITÁN (headwaiter)
22. CUCHARA (spoon)
23. PROPINA (tip)
24. PORCIÓN (portion)
25. RESERVA (reservation)
26. TENEDOR (fork)
27. VINAGRE (vinegar)
28. A LA CARTA (a la carte)
29. COCINERO (chef, cook)
30. CUBIERTO (table setting)
31. CUCHILLO (knife)
32. ENSALADA (salad)
33. ENTREMÉS (appetizer)
34. PIMIENTA (pepper [seasoning])
35. SERVICIO (service, service charge)
36. CAFETERÍA (cafeteria)
37. CUCHARITA (teaspoon)
38. POCO HECHO (rare [not well-done])
39. BIEN COCIDO (well-done)
40. SERVILLETA (napkin)

41. BUEN PROVECHO ("enjoy your meal!")
42. PLATO PRINCIPAL (entrée)
43. ACOMPAÑAMIENTO (side dish)
44. AYUDANTE DE CAMARERO (busboy)
45. ESPECIALIDAD DE LA CASA (house special)

Puzzle 44

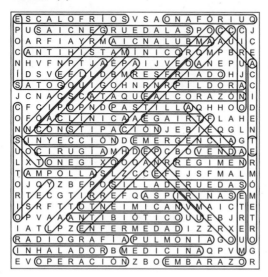

The words in the grid are: ACCIDENTE (accident), AMBULANCIA (ambulance), AMPOLLA (blister), ANTIBIÓTICO (antibiotic), ANTIHISTAMÍNICO (antihistamine), ASPIRINAS (aspirin), ATAQUE AL CORAZÓN (heart attack), CAMA (bed), CÁPSULA (capsule), CATARRO (chest cold), CIRUGÍA (surgery), CIRUJANO (surgeon), CLÍNICA (clinic), CONSTIPACIÓN (nasal congestion), CONSULTORIO (doctor's office), CURA (cure), DIETA (diet [selection]), DOLOR (ache), EMBARAZO (pregnancy), EMERGENCIA (emergency), ENFERMEDAD (illness/sickness), ENFERMERO (nurse), ENFERMO (ill/sick), ESCALOFRÍOS (chills), FIEBRE (fever), GOTAS (medicine drops), GRIPE (flu), HOSPITAL (hospital), INHALADOR (inhaler), INYECCIÓN (injection), LOCIÓN (lotion), MEDICINA (medicine), MÉDICO (doctor), MUERTE (death), NACIMIENTO (birth), OPERACIÓN (operation), OXÍGENO (oxygen), PACIENTE (patient), PASTILLA (tablet), PÍLDORA (pill), PULMONÍA (pneumonia), QUIRÓFANO (operating room), RADIOGRAFÍA (x-ray), RÉGIMEN (diet [plan]), RESFRIADO (head cold), SALA DE URGENCIAS (emergency room), SILLA DE RUEDAS (wheelchair), SÍNCOPE (fainting spell), SÍNTOMA (symptom), TERMÓMETRO (thermometer), TOS (cough), TRIAGE (triage), U.V.I. (abbreviation for I.C.U., which stands for UNIDAD DE VIGILANCIA INTENSIVA), VENDA (bandage), and YESO (plaster cast).

Puzzle 45

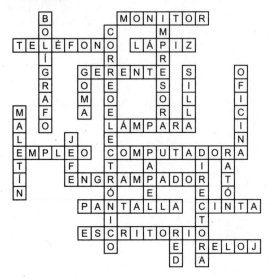

Puzzle 46

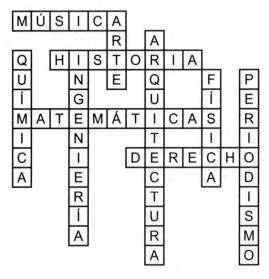

Puzzle 47

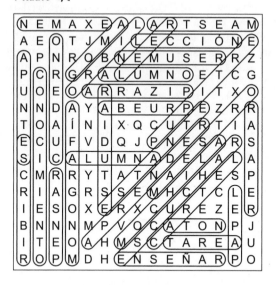

The 30 words, in alphabetical order, are: ALUMNA, ALUMNO, APRENDER, APUNTES, CARTEL, CONOCIMIENTO, CUADERNO, ENSEÑAR, ESCRIBIR, ESCUCHAR, ESTANTE, ESTUDIAR, EXAMEN, GOMA, LECCIÓN, LEER, LIBRO, MAESTRA, MAESTRO, MOCHILA, MONOGRAFÍA, NOTA, PAPEL, PENSAR, PIZARRA, PRUEBA, PUPITRE, REPASAR, RESUMEN, and TAREA.

Puzzle 48

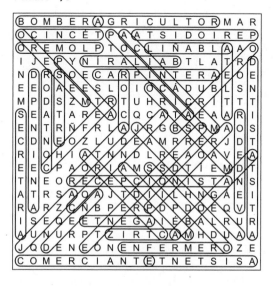

The 41 occupations in alphabetical order are: ABOGADA (lawyer), ACTOR (actor), ACTRIZ (actress), AGENTE (agent), AGRICULTOR (farmer), ALBAÑIL (mason), ARTISTA (artist), ASISTENTE (assistant), ATLETA (athlete), AUTOR (author), BAILARÍN (dancer), BARBERO (barber), BOMBERA (firefighter), CARPINTERA (carpenter), CARTERA (letter carrier), CHOFER (driver), COCINERA (chef), COMERCIANTE (businessperson), CONTADOR (accountant), DENTISTA (dentist), DEPENDIENTA (clerk), DUEÑA (business owner), ENFERMERO (nurse), JARDINERA (gardener/landscaper), JUEZA (judge), MAESTRO (teacher), MECÁNICA (mechanic), MÉDICA (physician), MESERO (waiter), PERIODISTA (journalist), PINTORA (painter), PLOMERO (plumber), POETA (poet), POLICÍA (police officer), PRESIDENTE (president), RECEPCIONISTA (receptionist), SASTRE (tailor), SECRETARIA (secretary), SOLDADO (soldier), TÉCNICO (technician), and VENDEDOR (salesperson).

Puzzle 49

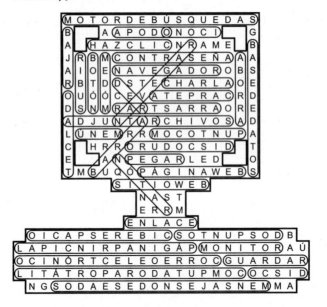

The words in the grid are: ADJUNTAR (attach [as a file]), APODO (screen name), ARCHIVOS (files), ARRASTRAR (drag), ARROBA (at sign [@]), BAJAR (download), BARRA (slash), BASE DE DATOS (database), BOTÓN (button), CARPETA (folder), CHARLA (chat), COMPUTADORA PORTÁTIL (laptop computer), CONTRASEÑA (password), CORREO ELECTRÓNICO (e-mail), CIBERESPACIO (cyberspace), DISCO (disk), DISCO DURO (hard drive), DOS PUNTOS (colon [in a Web address]), ENLACE (link), HAZ CLIC (click command), ICONO (icon), MENSAJES NO DESEADOS (spam), MENÚ (menu), MÓDEM (modem), MONITOR (monitor), MOTOR DE

BÚSQUEDAS (search engine), NAVEGADOR (browser), NAVEGAR (surf), PÁGINA PRINCIPAL (home page), PÁGINA WEB (Web page), PEGAR (bookmark [a Web site]), PUNTO COM (dot com), RATÓN (mouse), RED (Internet/network), SITIO WEB (Web site), SUBIR (upload), TECLADO (keyboard).

Puzzle 50

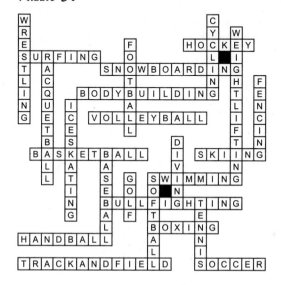

Puzzle 51

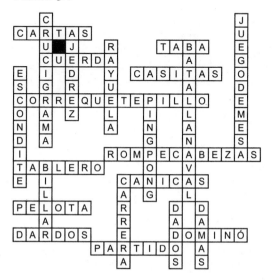

Puzzle 52

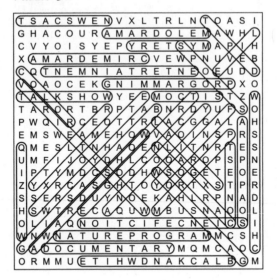

The 32 English words in the grid are: ANTHOLOGY (antología), AWARDS SHOW (espectáculo de premios), BLACK AND WHITE (blanco y negro), BROADCASTING (teledifusión), CARTOON (dibujo animado), CHILDREN'S SHOW (programa para niños), COLOR (color), CONTEST (concurso), CRIME DRAMA (historia policíaca), DOCUMENTARY (documental), ENTERTAINMENT (entretenimiento), FANTASY (fantasía), GAME SHOW (programa de juego), LIVE (en vivo), MELODRAMA (dramón), MYSTERY (misterio), NATURE PROGRAM (documental sobre la naturaleza), NEWSCAST (noticiero), PROGRAM (programa), PROGRAMMING (programación), QUIZ SHOW (programa de concurso), REALITY (telerealidad), SCIENCE FICTION (ciencia ficción), SERIAL (serial), SERMONETTE (sermón), SITCOM (comedia situacional), SOAP OPERA (telenovela), SPORTS (programa de deportes), TALK SHOW (programa de entrevistas), TAPED (grabado), TRAVELOGUE (documental de viaje), and VARIETY SHOW (espectáculo de variedades).

Puzzle 53

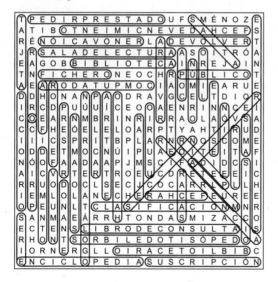

The words in the grid are: ARCHIVAR (file [verb]), ATLAS (atlas), BIBLIOTECA (library), BIBLIOTECARIA (librarian), CLASIFICACIÓN (classification), COMPUTADORA (computer), COPIA (photo-copy), DEPÓSITO DE LIBROS (book deposit), DEVOLVER (return [verb]), DICCIONARIO (dictionary), DOCUMENTO (document), DONANTE (donor), EDICIÓN (edition), EJEMPLAR (copy [of a book]), ENCICLOPEDIA (encyclopedia), ENTREGAR (turn in), ESTANTE (shelf), ESTANTERÍA (library stacks), ESTANTERÍA DE FICHEROS (card catalog), FECHA (date [noun]), FECHA DE VENCIMIENTO (due date), FECHADOR (date-stamp [noun]), FECHAR (date-stamp [verb]), FICHERO (library catalog), HACER PÚBLICO (issue [verb]), LECTOR (reader), LIBRO (book), LIBRO DE CONSULTA (reference book), MULTA (fine), NÚMERO (issue [noun]), NÚMERO DE CATÁLOGO (call number), ORDENAR (sort [verb]), PEDIR (request [verb]), PEDIR PRESTADO (borrow), PERIÓDICO (newspaper), PRESTAR (lend), PUBLICAR (publish), PÚBLICO (public), REFERENCIA (refer-ence), RENOVACIÓN (renewal), REVISTA (magazine), SACAR (take out [verb]), SALA DE LECTURA (reading room), SECCIÓN (section), SELLO TAMPÓN (rubber stamp), SERIE (series), SILENCIO (silence), SUMA (fee), SUSCRIPCIÓN (subscription), TARJETA (card), USUARIO (library patron), and VOLUMEN (volume).

Puzzle 54

1. PÓKER (poker)
2. RUMMY (rummy)
3. BRIDGE (bridge)
4. CANASTA (canasta)
5. OCHO LOCO (crazy eights)
6. SOLITARIO (solitaire)
7. VEINTIUNO (blackjack)
8. MUS
9. POZO
10. CHINCHÓN
11. CONTINENTAL

Puzzle 55

1. EL GRANATE (garnet)
2. LA AMATISTA (amethyst)
3. LA SANGUINARIA (bloodstone)
4. EL DIAMANTE (diamond)
5. LA ESMERALDA (emerald)
6. LA PERLA (pearl)
7. EL RUBÍ (ruby)
8. EL PERIDOTO (peridot)
9. EL ZAFIRO (sapphire)
10. EL ÓPALO (opal)
11. EL TOPACIO (topaz)
12. EL CIRCÓN (zircon)
13. EL LAPISLÁZULI (lapis lazuli)
14. LA CORNALINA (carnelian)
15. EL BERILO (beryl)
16. EL MARFIL (ivory)
17. LA AGUAMARINA (aquamarine)

Puzzle 56

1. CARA (face)
2. PESTAÑAS (eyelashes)
3. LENGUA (tongue)
4. DIENTES (teeth)
5. CEJAS (eyebrows)
6. LABIOS (lips)
7. FRENTE (forehead)
8. CUTIS (complexion)
9. OREJAS (outer ears)
10. BOCA (mouth)
11. NARIZ (nose)
12. OJOS (eyes)
13. OÍDOS (inner ears)
14. CABELLO (hair)

The additional word is CABEZA (head).

Puzzle 57

1. OJO (eye)
2. PIE (foot)
3. CODO (elbow)
4. CARA (face)
5. DEDO (finger)
6. MANO (hand)
7. BOCA (mouth)
8. CEJA (eyebrow)
9. PIEL (skin)
10. PELO (hair)
11. MUSLO (thigh)
12. NARIZ (nose)
13. LABIO (lip)
14. INGLE (groin)
15. BRAZO (arm)
16. PECHO (chest)
17. SANGRE (blood)
18. DIENTE (tooth)
19. CADERA (hip)
20. LENGUA (tongue)
21. PIERNA (leg)
22. CUELLO (neck)
23. RODILLA (knee)
24. TRASERO (buttocks)

25. CORAZÓN (heart)
26. ESPALDA (back)
27. NUDILLO (knuckle)
28. ESPINILLA (shin)
29. PANTORRILLA (calf)
30. OREJA (ear)
31. AXILA (armpit)
32. PULMÓN (lung)
33. MUÑECA (wrist)

34. FRENTE (forehead)
35. PESTAÑA (eyelash)
36. CEREBRO (brain)
37. CINTURA (waist)
38. COSTILLA (rib)
39. GARGANTA (throat)
40. ESTÓMAGO (stomach)
41. DEDO DEL PIE (toe)

Puzzle 58

The words in the grid are: ÁGUILA (eagle), ALCATRAZ (gannet), AVESTRUZ (ostrich), AZOR (hawk), BUHO (owl), BUITRE (vulture), CANARIO (canary), CIGÜEÑA (stork), CISNE (swan), COLIBRÍ (hummingbird), CUERVO (crow), FAISÁN (pheasant), GALLINA (hen), GALLO (rooster), GANSO (goose), GARZA (heron), GAVIOTA (seagull), GOLONDRINA (swallow), HALCÓN (falcon), LORO (parrot), PALOMA (dove), PATO (duck), PAVO (turkey), PERICO (parakeet), PINGÜINO (penguin), and POLLUELO (chick).

Puzzle 59

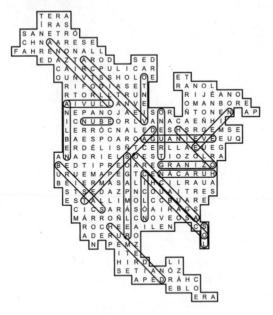

The 16 weather-related words in the map are: AGUACERO (downpour), AGUANIEVE (sleet), CHUBASCO (rainstorm), CICLÓN (cyclone), GRANIZO (hail), HIELO (ice), HUMEDAD (humidity), LLOVIZNA (drizzle), LLUVIA (rain), NEBLINA (mist), NIEVE (snow), NUBE (cloud), SOL (sun), TEMPESTAD (storm), VENTISCA (blizzard), and VIENTO (wind).

Puzzle 60

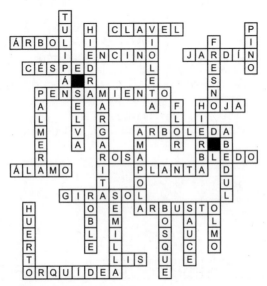

Puzzle 61

The hidden animals are: BALLENA (whale), CABALLO (horse), CABRA (goat), COCHINO (pig), CONEJO (rabbit), ELEFANTE (elephant), FOCA (seal), GATO (cat), GIRAFA (giraffe), LEÓN (lion), LOBO (wolf), MONO (monkey), MURCIÉLAGO (bat), OSO (bear), OVEJA (sheep), PÁJARO (bird), PERRO (dog), PEZ (fish), RANA (frog), RATA (rat), RATÓN (mouse), SAPO (toad), TIGRE (tiger), TOPO (mole), TORO (bull), TORTUGA (turtle), VACA (cow), VENADO (deer), and ZORRO (fox).

The hidden phrase is PARQUE ZOOLÓGICO (zoo).

Puzzle 62

Puzzle 63

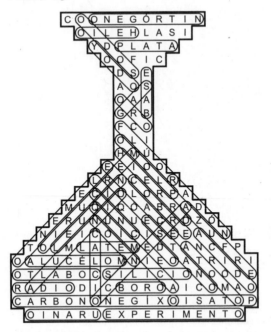

The 39 words in this grid are: ÁCIDO (acid), ALUMINIO (aluminum), ARSÉNICO (arsenic), ÁTOMO (atom), AZUFRE (sulfur), BASE (base), BORO (boron), CALCIO (calcium), CARBONO (carbon), CINC (zinc), COBALTO (cobalt), COBRE (copper), ELEMENTO (element), ENLACE (bond), ESTAÑO (tin), EXPERIMENTO (experiment), FLÚOR (fluorine), GAS (gas), HELIO (helium), HIERRO (iron), LÍQUIDO (liquid), MERCURIO (mercury), METAL (metal), MOLÉCULA (molecule), NEÓN (neon), NÍQUEL (nickel), NITRÓGENO (nitrogen), ORO (gold), OXÍGENO (oxygen), PLATA (silver), PLOMO (lead), POTASIO (potassium), QUÍMICA (chemistry), RADIO (radium), RADÓN (radon), SILICIO (silicon), SODIO (sodium), URANIO (uranium), and YODO (iodine).

The hidden phrase is CLASIFICACIÓN PERIÓDICA, which describes groupings on the periodic table of the elements.

Puzzle 64

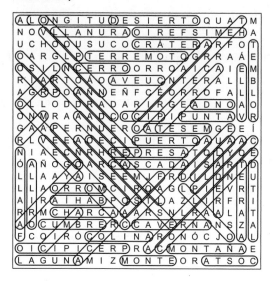

The words in the grid (and their translations) are: ARENA
(sand), ARROYO (stream), BAHÍA (bay), CABO (cape), CAÑÓN
(canyon), CASCADA (waterfall), CATARATA (waterfall [cataract]),
CAVERNA (cavern), CERRO (hill [in isolation]), CHARCA (pond),
CIÉNAGA (swamp), CIMA (summit), COLINA (hill [part of a chain]),
CORDILLERA (mountain range), CORRIENTE (current), COSTA
(coast), CRÁTER (crater), CUEVA (cave), CUMBRE (summit),
DESIERTO (desert), DIQUE (levee [dyke]), ECUADOR (equator),
ESTRECHO (strait), FARALLÓN (rocky promontory), FOSA (trench),
HEMISFERIO (hemisphere), ISLA (island), LADERA (slope), LAGO
(lake), LAGUNA (lagoon), LATITUD (latitude), LLANO (plain),
LLANURA (prairie), LOMA (knoll), LONGITUD (longitude), MAR (sea),
MESETA (plateau), MONTAÑA (mountain), MONTE (mountain [tree-
covered]), MORRO (hill [rocky point on coast]), OCÉANO (ocean),
OLA (wave [seawave]), ONDA (wave), ORILLA (shore), PASO (pass),
PEÑASCO (outcrop), PICO (peak), PIEDRA (stone), PLAYA (beach),
POLO (pole), PRECIPICIO (cliff), PUERTO (port), PUNTA (point),
REPRESA (reservoir), RÍO (river), ROCA (rock), SIERRA (mountain
range), TEMBLOR (tremor), TERRAZA (terrace), TERREMOTO
(earthquake), TERRITORIO (territory), TIERRA (land [earth]), VALLE
(valley), VEGA (treeless, empty plain), and VOLCÁN (volcano).

Puzzle 65

1. Will you be able to figure out all the answers to this puzzle? I hoPE SO! <u>PESO (México)</u>

2. A gonDOLA Ride is an enjoyable way to travel around Venice. <u>DÓLAR (El Salvador)</u>

3. Mascarpone cheese is what makes tiramiSU CREamy. <u>SUCRE (Bolivia)</u>

4. Louis PastEUR Originated the process of killing microbes in milk. <u>EURO (España)</u>

5. Fillings for a stromBOLI VARy from pepperoni to spinach. <u>BOLÍVAR (Venezuela)</u>

6. In ancient Rome, HanniBAL BOAsted of his military leadership. <u>BALBOA (Panamá)</u>

7. The protoCOL ON greeting a king or queen is to bow or curtsy to them. <u>COLÓN (Costa Rica)</u>

8. Because he had only four years in the Senate, the voting reCORD OBAma left before he became president was fairly sparse. <u>CÓRDOBA (Nicaragua)</u>

Puzzle 66

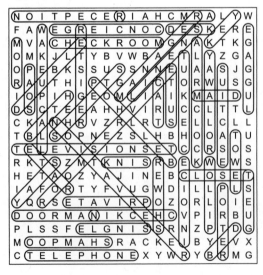

The words in the grid are: ALMOHADA (pillow), BAÑO (bath), BOTONES (bellhop), CAMA (bed), CAMA RODANTE (rollaway), CHAMPÚ (shampoo), CONSERJE (concierge), CONSIGNA (check-room), CRIADA (maid), DESPERTADOR (alarm clock), DOBLE (double), DUCHA (shower), EQUIPAJE (luggage), ESCRITORIO (desk), FACTURA (invoice), GERENTE/GERENTA (manager), HABITACIÓN (room), HÚESPED/HÚESPEDA (guest), IRSE (check out), JABÓN (soap), LAVABO (sink), LLAVE (key), MALETA (suitcase), MANTA (blanket), PERMANECER (stay [verb]), PORTAEQUIPAJES (cart), PORTERO (doorman), PRIVADO (private), RECEPCIÓN (reception), REGISTRARSE (check in), REGISTRO (register), RESERVA (reservation), ROPA BLANCA (linens), ROPERO (closet), SÁBANAS (sheets), SENCILLO (single), SERVICIO DE DESPERTADOR (wake-up call), SERVICIO DE HABITACIÓN (room service), SILLÓN (chair), SUITE (suite), TARIFA (rate), TELEVISOR (television set), TELÉFONO (telephone), and TOALLA (towel).

Puzzle 67

1. TOPE (speed bump)
2. ALTO (stop)
3. CURVA (curve)
4. PEAJE (toll)
5. CENTRO (downtown)
6. SALIDA (exit)
7. PELIGRO (danger)
8. PEATONES (pedestrians)
9. DESPACIO (slow)
10. SIN SALIDA (dead end)
11. CEDA EL PASO (yield)
12. ZONA DE CARGA (loading zone)
13. SENTIDO ÚNICO (one-way street)
14. VISTA DE INTERÉS (lookout point)
15. VELOCIDAD MÁXIMA (speed limit)
16. FERROCARRILES (railroad crossing)
17. PARADA DE AUTOBÚS (bus stop)
18. CAMINO CERRADO (road closed)
19. PUENTE LEVADIZO (drawbridge)
20. ENTRADA PROHIBIDA (do not enter)
21. ESTACIONAMIENTO (parking)
22. MANTENGA SU DERECHA (keep right)
23. MANTENGA SU IZQUIERDA (keep left)
24. PROHIBIDO CAMBIAR DE SENTIDO (no u-turn)
25. PROHIBIDO DOBLAR A LA DERECHA (no right turn)
26. PROHIBIDO DOBLAR A LA IZQUIERDA (no left turn)

Puzzle 68

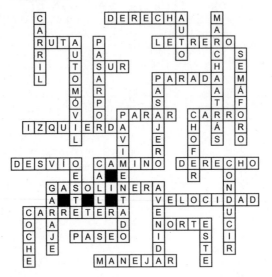

Puzzle 69

1. VÍA (track)
2. FILA (row)
3. BANCO (bench)
4. ANDÉN (platform)
5. VAGÓN (railroad car)
6. RELOJ (clock)
7. TÚNEL (tunnel)
8. SALIR (to depart)
9. SEÑAL (signal)
10. TARDE (late)
11. VIAJE (trip)
12. LAVABO (lavatory)
13. CAMINO (road)
14. SALIDA (departure)
15. LLEGAR (to arrive)
16. PASAJE (fare)
17. VIAJAR (to travel)
18. EXPRÉS (express)
19. ESPERAR (to wait)
20. QUIOSCO (newsstand)
21. LLEGADA (arrival)
22. VIAJERO (traveler)
23. VAGÓN COMEDOR (dining car)
24. HORARIO (schedule)
25. PASILLO (aisle)
26. LETRERO (sign)
27. ASIENTO (seat)
28. AUTOBÚS (bus)
29. RETRASO (delay)
30. BILLETE (ticket)
31. ANUNCIO (announcement)
32. ALTAVOZ (loudspeaker)
33. TEMPRANO (early)
34. EQUIPAJE (luggage)
35. PASAJERO (passenger)
36. GORRA ROJA (redcap)
37. COCHE-CAMA (sleeping car)
38. LOCOMOTORA (locomotive)
39. PASO A NIVEL (level crossing)
40. EQUIPAJE DE MANO (carry-on bag)
41. SALA DE ESPERA (waiting room)
42. TAQUILLA DE VENTA (ticket counter)
43. CARRITO DE EQUIPAJE (luggage cart)
44. CASETA DE INFORMACIÓN (information booth)
45. ESTACIÓN DE AUTOBÚS (bus station)
46. ESTACIÓN DE FERROCARRIL (train station)
47. ALTA VELOCIDAD ESPAÑOLA (AVE train)

Puzzle 70

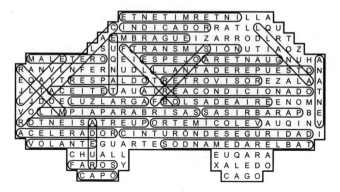

The 34 words in the diagram are: ACEITE (oil), ACELERADOR (gas pedal), AIRE ACONDICIONADO (air conditioning), ASIENTO (seat), BOLSA DE AIRE (air bag), CALENTADOR (heater), CAPÓ (hood), CINTURÓN DE SEGURIDAD (safety belt), EMBRAGUE (clutch), ESPEJO (mirror), FAROS (headlights), FILTRO (filter), FRENOS (brakes), GUANTERA (glove compartment), INDICADOR (gauge), INTERMITENTE (turn signal), LIMPIAPARABRISAS (windshield wipers), LLANTA (tire), LLANTA DE REPUESTO (spare tire), LLAVE (key), LUZ LARGA (high beams), MALETERO (trunk), MOTOR (engine), PARABRISAS (windshield), PUERTA (door), RESPALDO (back rest), RETROVISOR (rear-view mirror), RUEDA (wheel), TABLERA DE MANDOS (dashboard), TANQUE (gas tank), TRANSMISIÓN (transmission), VELOCÍMETRO (speedometer), VENTANA (window), and VOLANTE (steering wheel).

Puzzle 71

1. CHILE (LECHE)
2. BOLIVIA (OLIVIA)
3. PARAGUAY (PARAGUAS)
4. NICARAGUA (CARA)
5. URUGUAY (U->E, R->L, G->M, A->N, Y ->T)
6. ARGENTINA (TANGERINE)
7. MEXICO (MÉDICO)
8. PERU (PURE)
9. HONDURAS (THOUSAND)
10. SPAIN (SPIN/NIPS; SPAN/NAPS)

Puzzle 72

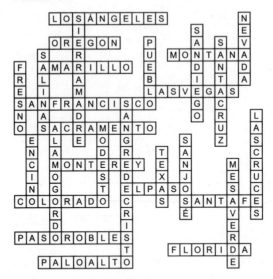

Names and translations in alphabetical order: ALAMOGORDO (big poplar), AMARILLO (yellow), COLORADO (red), EL PASO (the pass), ENCINO (live oak), FLORIDA (flowery), FRESNO (ash tree), LAS CRUCES (the crosses), LAS VEGAS (treeless, empty plain), LOS ÁNGELES (the angels), MESA VERDE (green butte), MODESTO (modest), MONTANA (mountain), MONTEREY (king's mountain), NEVADA (snowy), OREGON (from *orejón,* big ears), PALO ALTO (tall tree), PASO ROBLES (oak pass), PUEBLO (town), SACRAMENTO (sacrament), SALINAS (salt marshes), SAN DIEGO (Saint James), SAN FRANCISCO (Saint Francis), SAN JOSÉ (Saint Joseph), SANGRE DE CRISTO (blood of Christ), SANTA CRUZ (holy cross), SANTA FE (holy faith), SIERRA MADRE (mother range), and TEXAS (tiles).

Puzzle 73

1. EL BRASIL (Brazil)
2. ITALIA (Italy)
3. RUSIA (Russia)
4. GRECIA (Greece)
5. POLONIA (Poland)
6. INGLATERRA (England)
7. FRANCIA (France)

8. SUDÁFRICA (South Africa)
9. TURQUÍA (Turkey)
10. LOS ESTADOS UNIDOS (The United States)
11. AFGANISTÁN (Afghanistan)
12. ALEMANIA (Germany)
13. EL CANADÁ (Canada)
14. LAS FILIPINAS (The Philippines)
15. TAILANDIA (Thailand)
16. PAQUISTÁN (Pakistan)
17. ESCOCIA (Scotland)
18. EGIPTO (Egypt)
19. ARABIA SAUDITA (Saudi Arabia)
20. NORUEGA (Norway)
21. IRLANDA (Ireland)
22. IRAK (Iraq)
23. EL JAPÓN (Japan)
24. KENIA (Kenya)
25. SUECIA (Sweden)
26. GALES (Wales)
27. FINLANDIA (Finland)
28. JORDANIA (Jordan)
29. DINAMARCA (Denmark)

Puzzle 74

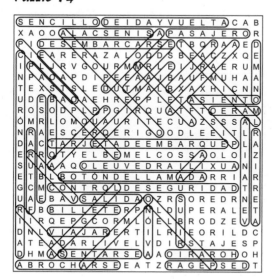

Puzzle 75

1. ARROZ	14. TAPAS	26. JIBARITOS
2. BURRITOS	15. AJIACO	27. LECHÓN
3. CHIMICHANGAS	16. AREPAS	28. MOROS Y
4. EMPANADAS	17. ARROZ CON	CRISTIANOS (black
5. ENCHILADAS	GANDULES	beans and rice)
6. FAJITAS	18. BANDEJA PAISA	29. PABELLÓN
7. FRIJOLES	19. CARNE ASADA	30. PARRILLADA
8. GUACAMOLE	20. CAZUELA	31. PUPUSAS
9. MOLE	21. CEVICHE	32. SANCOCHO
10. PAELLA	22. CHIVITO	33. SERRANO
11. PICO DE GALLO	23. CUY	34. TACOS AL PASTOR
12. TACOS	24. GALLO PINTO	35. TAPADO
13. TAMALES	25. HUMINTAS	

Puzzle 76

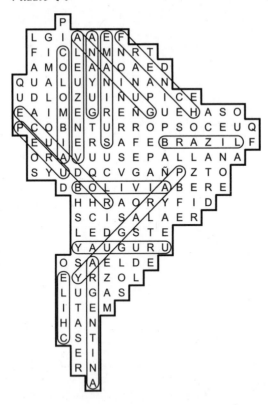

The countries, in alphabetical order, are ARGENTINA, BOLIVIA, BRAZIL, CHILE, COLOMBIA, ECUADOR, FRENCH GUIANA, GUYANA, PARAGUAY, PERU, SURINAME, URUGUAY, and VENEZUELA. The country names are in the grid in their approximate location on the map.

Puzzle 77

1. MIGUEL DE CERVANTES
2. JORGE LUIS BORGES
3. JUNOT DÍAZ (AUTOR)
4. PLÁCIDO DOMINGO
5. JOSÉ CARRERAS
6. MONTSERRAT CABALLÉ (CANTANTE)
7. PENÉLOPE CRUZ
8. SALMA HAYEK
9. RITA MORENO (ACTRIZ)
10. ERNESTO "CHE" GUEVARA
11. FIDEL CASTRO
12. PANCHO VILLA (REVOLUCIONARIO)
13. ALBERTO SALAZAR
14. ROBERTO CLEMENTE
15. SEVE BALLESTEROS (ATLETA)

Puzzle 78

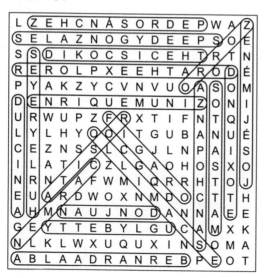

The 19 fictional characters in the puzzle are: BERNARDA ALBA
(theater), CARMEN (opera), DON JUAN (literature/theater/poetry),
DON QUIXOTE (literature), DORA THE EXPLORER (television),
DULCINEA (literature), ENRIQUE MUNIZ (television), ESCAMILLO
(opera), FIGARO (opera), HURLEY REYES (television), JOSÉ
JIMÉNEZ (television), MATT SANTOS (television), PEDRO SÁNCHEZ
(movies), ROSITA (television), SANCHO PANZA (literature), SPEEDY
GONZALES (cartoons), THE CISCO KID (television/radio/movies),
UGLY BETTY (television), and ZORRO (literature/television/movies).

Puzzle 79

```
              H               R
  M É X I C O         P       E
              N       U       P A N A M Á
              D     P E R Ú
              U       R       B
              R       T               N
              A       O       I   C H I L E
  V       E   C O S T A R I C A         C
  E       L   U           I   A         A
  N       S   B           C   D         R
  E S P A Ñ A         C O L O M B I A     U
  Z       L                   M   O   G   R
  U       V                   I   L   U   U
  E C U A D O R   A R G E N T I N A     G   U
  L       D                   I   V     U
  A       O                   C   I     A
          R                 P A R A G U A Y
                              N
    G U A T E M A L A
```

Puzzle 80

1. PEOR ES NADA.
   (Half a loaf is better than none.)
2. PERSEVERA Y TRIUNFIRÁS.
   (Never say die.)
3. EN ABRIL, AGUAS MIL.
   (April showers bring May flowers.)
4. A MAL TIEMPO, BUENA CARA.
   (Let a smile be your umbrella.)
5. EL QUE NO LLORA, NO MAMA.
   (The squeaky wheel gets the grease.)
6. ENTRE BUEYES NO HAY CORNADAS.
   (There is no honor among thieves.)
7. CUANDO HAY HAMBRE, NO HAY PAN DURO.
   (Beggars can't be choosers.)
8. CRÍA CUERVOS Y TE SACARÁN LOS OJOS.
   (Lie down with dogs and you wake up with fleas.)
9. ANTES QUE TE CASES, MIRA LO QUE HACES.
   (Look before you leap.)
10. NO SE GANÓ ZAMORA EN UNA HORA.
    (Rome wasn't built in a day.)
11. OJOS QUE NO VEN, CORAZÓN QUE NO LLORA.
    (Out of sight, out of mind.)
12. DEL DICHO AL HECHO, HAY MUCHO TRECHO.
    (Talk is cheap.)

Puzzle 81

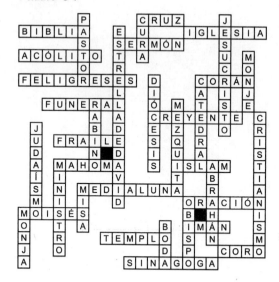

Puzzle 82

1. MEXICANO
2. DOMINICANA
3. PANAMEÑA
4. PERUANO
5. CHILENA
6. ARGENTINO
7. BOLIVIANO
8. ECUATORIANO
9. URUGUAYO
10. PARAGUAYO
11. COLOMBIANA
12. CUBANA
13. HONDUREÑA
14. VENEZOLANO
15. PUERTORRIQUEÑA
16. SALVADOREÑO
17. ESPAÑOLA
18. ECUATOGUINEANA
19. NICARAGÜENSE
20. GUATEMALTECA
21. COSTARRICENSE

The hidden phrase is IDENTITY CRISIS.

Puzzle 83

The 25 terms are: ANDALUZA (Andalucía, España), ARAGONÉS (Aragón, España), BARCELONESA (Barcelona, España), BOGOTANO (Bogotá, Colombia), BURGALESA (Burgos, España), CAPITALINA (México, D.F., México), CARAQUEÑO (Caracas, Venezuela), CASTELLANO (Castilla, España), CATALANA (Cataluña, España), CHIHUAHUENSE (Chihuahua, México), CORDOBÉS (Córdoba, España), EXTREMEÑA (Extremadura, España), GALLEGO (Galicia, España), GRANADINA (Granada, España), GUANTANAMERO (Guántanamo, Cuba), HABANERO (La Habana, Cuba), LIMEÑA (Lima, Perú), MADRILEÑO (Madrid, España), MALAGUEÑO (Málaga, España), PORTEÑO (Buenos Aires, Argentina), RÍOPLATENSE (Río de la Plata, Argentina/Uruguay), SEVILLANA (Sevilla, España), TAPATÍO (Guadalajara, México), TOLEDANA (Toledo, España), and VASCA (País Vasco, España).

Puzzle 84

1. LA BELLA Y LA BESTIA (Beauty and the Beast)
2. DEDOS DE ORO (Goldfinger)
3. GUERRAS DE LAS GALAXIAS (Star Wars)
4. LAS UVAS DE LA IRA (The Grapes of Wrath)
5. HOMBRES DE NEGRO (Men in Black)
6. CUENTA CONMIGO (Stand by Me)
7. EL SEÑOR DE LOS ANILLOS (The Lord of the Rings)
8. ¡QUÉ BELLO ES VIVIR! (It's a Wonderful Life)
9. BUENOS MUCHACHOS (Goodfellas)

10. LOS CAZADORES DEL ARCA PERDIDA (Raiders of the Lost Ark)
11. LO QUE EL VIENTO SE LLEVÓ (Gone with the Wind)
12. LOS MEJORES AÑOS DE NUESTRA VIDA (The Best Years of Our Lives)

Puzzle 85

The words in the grid for which there are English translations are:
AVENTURA (adventure), BÚSQUEDA (quest), CABALLERÍA (chivalry),
CABALLERO ANDANTE (knight errant), CABALLO (horse), ESCUDERO
(squire), ESCUDO (shield), HIDALGO (landowner/nobleman),
INGENIOSO (clever/ingenious/inventive), LANZA (lance), MOLINO DE
VIENTO (windmill), MULA (mule), and VENTERO (innkeeper).

Puzzle 86

1. REY
2. DAMA
3. BARÓN
4. CONDE
5. SEÑOR
6. NOBLE
7. REINA
8. VIRREY
9. CONDESA
10. REALEZA
11. BARONESA
12. HEREDERO
13. PRÍNCIPE
14. PRINCESA
15. EMBAJADOR
16. EMPERADOR
17. CABALLERO
18. EMPERATRIZ
19. ARISTÓCRATA
20. DAMA DE HONOR

Puzzle 87

1. SELENA
2. EVA PERÓN
3. CANTINFLAS
4. FRIDA KAHLO
5. JOSÉ FERRER
6. CÉSAR CHÁVEZ
7. PABLO CASALS
8. SEVERO OCHOA
9. SIMÓN BOLÍVAR
10. BENITO JUÁREZ
11. PABLO PICASSO
12. SALVADOR DALÍ
13. ANDRÉS SEGOVIA
14. JUNÍPERO SERRA
15. PALOMA PICASSO
16. CRISTÓBAL COLÓN
17. PEDRO ALMODÓVAR
18. SANDRA CISNEROS
19. SONIA SOTOMAYOR
20. ALFONSINA STORNI
21. CAROLINA HERRERA
22. GABRIELA MISTRAL
23. JUAN PONCE DE LEÓN
24. RODRIGO DÍAZ DE VIVAR
    ("EL CID")
25. ARANTXA SÁNCHEZ VICARIO

Puzzle 88

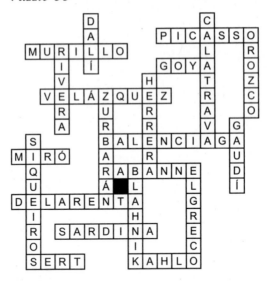

Puzzle 89

1. ISABEL ALLENDE
2. GUSTAVO ADOLFO BÉCQUER
3. JORGE LUIS BORGES
4. MIGUEL DE CERVANTES
   SAAVEDRA
5. JULIO CORTÁZAR
6. RUBÉN DARÍO
7. CARLOS FUENTES
8. FEDERICO GARCÍA LORCA
9. GABRIEL GARCÍA MARQUEZ
10. LOPE DE VEGA
11. JOSÉ MARTÍ
12. PABLO NERUDA
13. OCTAVIO PAZ
14. BENITO PÉREZ GALDÓS
15. JUAN RULFO
16. MARIO VARGAS LLOSA

Puzzle 90

1. LEÓN, NICARAGUA
2. CALI, COLOMBIA
3. COLÓN, PANAMÁ
4. CUZCO, PERÚ
5. PONCE, PUERTO RICO
6. SALTO, URUGUAY
7. ANTIGUA, GUATEMALA
8. CÓRDOBA, ARGENTINA
9. SANTA ANA, EL SALVADOR
10. BARCELONA, ESPAÑA
11. BOCA CHICA, REPÚBLICA DOMINICANA
12. GUAYAQUIL, ECUADOR
13. MARACAIBO, VENEZUELA
14. COCHABAMBA, BOLIVIA
15. CONCEPCIÓN, PARAGUAY
16. GUANTÁNAMO, CUBA
17. VALPARAÍSO, CHILE
18. GUADALAJARA, MÉXICO
19. PUERTO LIMÓN, COSTA RICA
20. SAN PEDRO SULA, HONDURAS

Puzzle 91

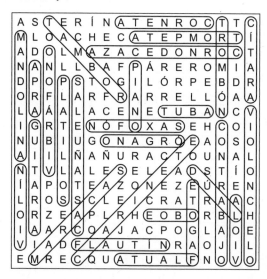

The 27 instruments, in alphabetical order, are: ARPA (harp), CASTAÑUELAS (castanets), CÍTARA (zither), CLARINETE (clarinet), CONTRABAJO (bass violin), CORNETA (cornet), CORNO DE CAZA (French horn), FAGOTE (bassoon), FLAUTA (flute), FLAUTÍN (piccolo), GUITARRA (guitar), LAÚD (lute), MANDOLINA (mandolin), MARACAS (maracas), OBOE (oboe), ÓRGANO (organ), PIANO (piano), PLATILLOS (cymbals), SAXOFÓN (saxophone), TAMBOR (drum), TROMBÓN (trombone), TROMPETA (trumpet), TUBA (tuba), VIBRÁFONO (vibes), VIOLA (viola), VIOLÍN (violin), and VIOLONCHELO (cello).

Puzzle 92

1. OÍDO (heard)
2. ROTO (broken)
3. LEÍDO (read)
4. DICHO (said)
5. HECHO (done, made)
6. VISTO (seen)
7. MUERTO (died)
8. PUESTO (put)

9. TRAÍDO (brought)
10. VUELTO (turned)
11. ABIERTO (opened)
12. ESCRITO (written)
13. IMPRESO (printed)
14. CUBIERTO (covered)
15. RESUELTO (resolved)
16. DESCUBIERTO (discovered)

Puzzle 93

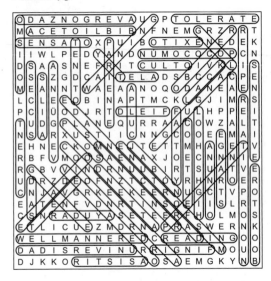

1. ACTUAL (VERDADERO)/ACTUAL (CURRENT)
2. ADVERTISEMENT (ANUNCIO)/ADVERTENCIA (WARNING)
3. ARENA (ESTADIO)/ARENA (SAND)
4. (TO) ASSIST (AYUDAR)/ASISTIR (ATTEND)
5. (TO) ATTEND (ASISTIR)/ATENDER (TEND TO)
6. CAMP (CAMPAMENTO)/CAMPO (FIELD)
7. COLLEGE (UNIVERSIDAD)/COLEGIO (HIGH SCHOOL)
8. DISGRACE (VERGÜENZA)/DESGRACIA (MISFORTUNE)
9. EDUCATED (CULTO)/EDUCADO (WELL-MANNERED)
10. EMBARRASSED (AVERGONZADO)/EMBARAZADA (PREGNANT)
11. EXIT (SALIDA)/ÉXITO (SUCCESS)
12. FABRIC (TELA)/FÁBRICA (FACTORY)
13. FAULT (CULPA)/FALTA (LACK)
14. IDIOM (MODISMO)/IDIOMA (LANGUAGE)
15. LARGE (GRANDE)/LARGO (LONG)
16. LECTURE (CONFERENCIA)/LECTURA (READING)

17. LIBRARY (BIBLIOTECA)/LIBRERÍA (BOOKSTORE)
18. (TO) PRETEND (FINGIR)/PRETENDER (TRY)
19. RARE (POCO COMÚN)/RARO (STRANGE)
20. (TO) REALIZE (DARSE CUENTA DE)/REALIZAR (COME TRUE)
21. RECEIPT (RECIBO)/RECETA (RECIPE)
22. RELATIVE (PARIENTE)/RELATIVO (RELATIVE PRONOUN)
23. SENSIBLE (SENSATO)/SENSIBLE (SENSITIVE)
24. SOAP (JABÓN)/SOPA (SOUP)
25. (TO) SUPPORT (MANTENER)/SOPORTAR (TOLERATE)
26. SUCCESS (ÉXITO)/SUCESO (EVENT)

Puzzle 94

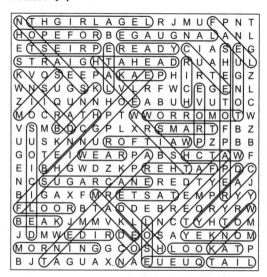

The words in the grid (with their Spanish equivalents in parentheses) are: BANK, BENCH (banco); FISHING POLE, SUGAR CANE (caña); QUEUE, TAIL (cola); LEGAL RIGHT, STRAIGHT AHEAD (derecho); HOPE FOR, WAIT FOR (esperar); DEPOT, SEASON (estación); DO, MAKE (hacer); LEAF, SHEET OF PAPER (hoja); LANGUAGE, TONGUE (lengua); READY, SMART (listo)*; CARRY, WEAR (llevar); MORNING, TOMORROW (mañana); LOOK AT, WATCH (mirar); CUTE, MONKEY (mono); DOLL, WRIST (muñeca); FATHER, PRIEST (padre); LOSE, MISS (perder); BEAK, PEAK (pico); APARTMENT, FLOOR [STORY OF A BUILDING] (piso); PROVE, TRY (probar); DELICIOUS, RICH (rico); KNOW, TASTE (saber); AFTERNOON, LATE (tarde); HAVE, HOLD (tener); and DRINK, RIDE (tomar).

* LISTO means READY with the verb ESTAR and SMART with the verb SER.

Puzzle 95

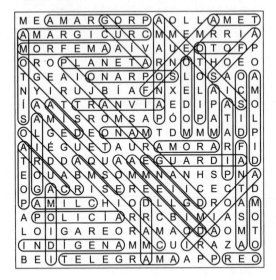

The 46 words in the grid are, in alphabetical order: AROMA (aroma), CARISMA (charisma), CLIMA (climate), CRUCIGRAMA (crossword puzzle), CURA (priest), DÍA (day), DIAGRAMA (diagram), DILEMA (dilemma), DIPLOMA (diploma), DISCO (discotheque), DRAMA (drama), ENIGMA (enigma), ESQUEMA (outline), FANTASMA (ghost), FONEMA (phoneme), FOTO (photograph), GORILA (gorilla), GUARDIA (guard/officer), GUÍA (male guide), IDIOMA (language), IDIOTA (idiot), INDÍGENA (native), MANO (hand), MAPA (map), MODELO (female model), MORFEMA (morpheme), MOTO (motorcycle), PANORAMA (panorama), PIJAMA (pajamas), PILOTO (female pilot), PIRATA (pirate), PLANETA (planet), POETA (male poet), POLICÍA (male police officer), PROBLEMA (problem), PROGRAMA (program), RADIO (radio transmission), REO (female convict), SÍNTOMA (symptom), SISTEMA (system), SOFÁ (sofa), SOPRANO (soprano), TELEGRAMA (telegram), TEMA (theme), TESTIGO (female witness), and TRANVÍA (streetcar).

Puzzle 96

1. Mary HAD A little lamb. (FAIRY)
2. Ana thanked the host for A VEry nice evening. (BIRD)
3. Violeta Chamorro was the first female president of NicarAGUA. (WATER)
4. José bought a large-screen plASMA television for the den. (ASTHMA)
5. JeAN-CLAude Van Damme starred in the movie "Double Impact." (ANCHOR)
6. CabÁGUIL and Acan were two Mayan gods. (EAGLE)
7. The meat sandwich was made with HAM, BREad, and mustard. (HUNGER)
8. The bank teller asked me to sign the check witH A BLAck pen. (SPEECH [manner of speaking])
9. We danced the rumba, tango, and cHACHA at the dance marathon. (AXE)
10. "We can't go to Cuba and not visit the capital, La HABAna," said Olga to the travel agent. (BEAN)
11. "Have you seen any of the plays by Honoré de [B]ALZAc?" (INCREASE/RISE)
12. The plane spent 30 minutes on the tARMAc after taxiing. (WEAPON)
13. Rosa's favorite song was "Diamonds ÁRE A Girl's Best Friend." (AREA)
14. "That comedy movie was so funny; it was a reAL GAs!" (SEAWEED)
15. Miguel aptly named his new dALMAtian "Spot." (SOUL)
16. Francisco's favorite judge on "American Idol" was [P]AULA Abdul. (CLASSROOM)
17. Rita forgot to buy ASPAragus from the greengrocer. (CROSS)
18. The student's short attention span made him very distrACTAble. (ACT)
19. Abuelita used to enjoy watching Ricardo MontALBAn on "Fantasy Island." (DAWN)
20. Héctor walked along the EmbARCAdero when he visited San Francisco. (CHEST/BOX)
21. Pedro didn't want the dinner special, so he ordered from the A LA cARTE menu. (WING/ART)

Puzzle 97

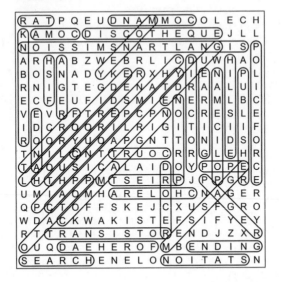

The words in the grid, in alphabetical order, are: ANGER (la cólera), ANODE (el terminal), CAPITAL CITY (la capital), CHAMPIONSHIP (la final), CHOLERA (el cólera), COMA (el coma), COMMA (la coma), COMMAND (el orden), COURT (la corte), CURE (la cura), CUT (el corte), DIRECTORY (la guía), DISCOTHEQUE (la disco), EARRING (el pendiente), EDITORIAL (el editorial), ENDING (el final), FISH (el pez), FOREHEAD (la frente), FRONT (el frente), GUIDE (el guía), HILLSIDE (la pendiente), HOLY ORDER (la orden), MARGIN (el margen), MESSAGE (el parte), MONEY (el capital), PAGER (el busca), POLICE FORCE (la policía), POLICEMAN (el policía), POPE (el papa), PORTION (la parte), POTATO (la papa), PRIEST (el cura), PUBLISHER (la editorial), RECORD (el disco), RIVERBANK (la margen), SEARCH (la busca), SIGNAL TRANSMISSION (la radio), STATION (la terminal), TAR (la pez), and TRANSISTOR (el radio).

Puzzle 98

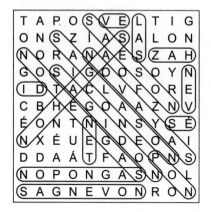

The commands are DI, NO DIGAS (DECIR); HAZ, NO HAGAS (HACER); VE, NO VAYAS (IR); PON, NO PONGAS (PONER); SAL, NO SALGAS (SALIR); SÉ, NO SEAS (SER); TEN, NO TENGAS (TENER); and VEN, NO VENGAS (VENIR).

Puzzle 99

1. HARÉ (HACER)
2. DIRÁN (DECIR)
3. HABRÉ (HABER)
4. SALDRÉ (SALIR)
5. TENDRÁ (TENER)

6. VENDRÉ (VENIR)
7. VALDRÁ (VALER)
8. PONDRÁ (PONER)
9. PODRÁN (PODER)
10. CABRÁS (CABER)

Puzzle 100

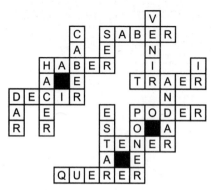

Puzzle 101

1. DIRÍA (DECIR)
2. CABRÍA (CABER)
3. HARÍAS (HACER)
4. HABRÍAN (HABER)
5. PODRÍAN (PODER)

6. PONDRÍA (PONER)
7. SALDRÍA (SALIR)
8. VALDRÍA (VALER)
9. VENDRÍAS (VENIR)
10. TENDRÍAS (TENER)

Puzzle 102

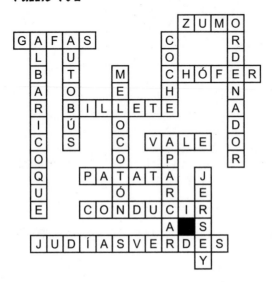

Castilian	*Latin American*
1. CHÓFER	CHOFER
2. ALBARICOQUE	DAMASCO
3. AUTOBÚS	GUAGUA
4. COCHE	CARRO
5. ORDENADOR	COMPUTADORA
6. CONDUCIR	MANEJAR
7. GAFAS	LENTES
8. ZUMO	JUGO
9. JUDÍAS VERDES	HABICHUELAS
10. VALE	DE ACUERDO
11. APARCAR	ESTACIONAR
12. MELOCOTÓN	DURAZNO
13. PATATA	PAPA
14. JERSEY	SUÉTER
15. BILLETE	BOLETO

Puzzle 103

1. KIWI	14. KUWAIT
2. KALEIDOSCOPIO	15. WAFLERO
3. KARATE	16. WALKIRIA
4. KARTING	17. WAPITÍ
5. KAYAC	18. WÁTER
6. KENIA	19. WATERPOLO
7. KILO	20. WEB
8. KIMONO	21. WEBCAM
9. KINDERGARTEN	22. WÉLTER
10. KINESIOLOGÍA	23. WHISKY
11. KIOSKO	24. WINDSURFING
12. KOSHER	25. WINDSURFISTA
13. KRIPTÓN	26. WOLFRAMIO

Part IV
The Part of Tens

The 5th Wave   By Rich Tennant

"I've always found my Spanish improves with
a little practice, some study, and about
3 or 4 margaritas."

In this part...

*H*ere we offer you some meatier, mind-stretching puzzles to incorporate all the vocabulary and solving savvy you can muster. And we give you some pointers, field-tested on thousands of language students over the years, on how to maintain, sharpen, and even improve on what you've achieved so far with your talents in Spanish.

Chapter 11

Ten Challenger Puzzles

Puzzle 1: Three of a Kind

If you insert the word ORO into the letter strings AMSO, CNEL, and TNJA, you can form the words AMOROSO, CORONEL, and TORONJA. For each example, find the three-letter Spanish word that can be inserted into each of the three letter strings to form longer Spanish words. The three-letter word may be inserted anywhere in the sequence, not necessarily in the middle as in the example.

1. VILLETA MEO CONVACIÓN   _____

2. CAERO AILLO TES   _____

3. BAA FISTA MEADO   _____

4. COTIBLE CUBREA ONCILLO   _____

5. ARIO ENADA UD   _____

6. TAL DETES OTUNA   _____

7. GULAR CAMPEO AGOGA   _____

8. DOSCIEN COSO OCOPIO   _____

9. CAMA TALLA EMADA   _____

10. BOS RIZA SO   _____

Puzzle 2: Four by Four (by Two)

Here we give you two puzzles for the price of one. These 4x4 grids look deceptively easy, but we've combined the two sets of clues into one and arranged the clues in random order with their corresponding numbers. Both the clues and the answers are in Spanish. Figuring out which words fit in each grid is up to you.

Hint: One of the words in this puzzle has a property shared by very few words in Spanish. Can you figure out what it is?

Across

1 NÚMERO DE DÍAS DE NAVIDAD
   MÁQUINA PARA MIRAR PROGRAMAS

5 TIEMPOS DE REVOLUCIONES DE PLANETAS
   PREMIOS PARA GANADORES EN LOS JUEGOS OLÍMPICOS

6 NADA
   PATATA DULCE ANARANJADA

7 ANIMALES FEROCES
   PARTES DE PÁJAROS QUE LES PERMITEN VOLAR

Down

1 TÍTULO PARA UNA MUJER
   TORTILLA RELLENA

2 LETRAS CON TILDES
   HABLADO

3 PÁJARO QUE HABLA
   SÍMBOLO DE PUNCTUACIÓN PARA PAUSAR

4 LETRAS PARA PLURALIZAR
   PRONOMBRE DEMOSTRATIVO PLURAL

1	2	3	4
5			
6			
7			

1	2	3	4
5			
6			
7			

Puzzle 3: Block Letters

Use the letters in this 3x3 grid to form words that define the clues below. The letters may appear in any order and do not necessarily have to connect from one square to an adjacent one. Although the letters A and L repeat, no individual square may be used more than once. As a hint, the correct answers are listed in alphabetical order within each section.

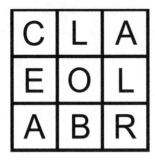

4 Letters

ABERTURA QUE TIENE LA LENGUA Y LOS DIENTES
ALQUITRÁN O RESINA DEL PINO
PUNTA DE TIERRA
COSTOSO
FRENTE DE LA CABEZA
TRABAJO
CACEROLA PARA COCINAR
PIEDRA DURA

5 Letters

NAVE
BONITO
ACOMODAR EN UN ESPACIO
DONDE PASAN CAMINANTES O VEHÍCULOS
ANIMAL BLANCO Y NEGRO
EVIDENTE O LUMINOSO
CLASE DE SERPIENTE
METAL DE PENIQUES
ÁRBOL QUE SIMBOLIZA LA FUERZA

6 Letters

ADORNO PARA EL CUELLO

7 Letters

ANIMAL PARA MONTAR
PELO
BULBO QUE PRODUCE LÁGRIMAS

9 Letters

DON QUIJOTE O EL CID, POR EJEMPLO

Puzzle 4: At First Sight

You can identify the 30 words in this word search grid by the clues listed below, with one hitch: The words described by the clues differ from those in the grid by their first letter. For example, the answer to the first clue is JUEGO, and so the word to look for in the grid is FUEGO. Can you figure out all the words defined by their clues and their counterparts in the grid?

```
N B R H O P I N T A A A O
U L I U H O M B R E D S S
E M C E O C O F Í A O E A
Z U A S N T U D H I N R C
N E L O O E O A O F A B A
O R O M N L L Ñ H U S O M
C T R T O L E E C E I S I
H O E R I T O Z E G E C C
E E D V N I L J P O R O P
E G T E L E F U A A R R A
S U L R I E N T E A A T P
O F Á M A R C A R H C E A
A H C U L P S O Ñ E U D L
```

1. ACTIVIDAD PARA DIVERTIRSE   _____

2. ALGUIEN QUE DECIDE LA LEY   _____

3. ALTERNATIVO DE BAÑO   _____

4. ATRAVIESA UN RÍO O CAMINO   _____

5. AUTOMÓVIL   _____

6. AZUL O VERDE, POR EJEMPLO   _____

7. CEREBRO   _____

8. CÓMO ALGUIEN SE LLAMA   _____

9. CONTIENE CINCO DEDOS   _____

10. COSTOSO   _____

11. CUARTO PLANETA DEL SOL   _____

12. DECORACIÓN PARA UN REGALO   _____

13. IMAGEN PRODUCIDA POR
UNA CÁMARA   _____

14. IMÁGENES MIENTRAS SE DUERME   _____

15. INDICA LOCACIÓN O
DIRECCIÓN   _____

16. LO QUE COMEN LOS RATONES   _____

17. LUGAR PARA SENTARSE   _____

18. MASTICA LA COMIDA   _____

19. NAVE   _____

20. NO RICO   _____

21. NUESTRO PLANETA   _____

22. NÚMERO DE CENTAVOS
EN UN DÓLAR   _____

23. OPUESTO DE SUR   _____

24. OPUESTO DE TODO   _____

25. ÓRGANO PARA VER   _____

26. PUEBLO CERCA DEL MAR   _____

27. RECIPIENTE DE BEBIDA   _____

28. SONIDO SIMILAR EN UN POEMA   _____

29. TEJADO DE UN EDIFICIO   _____

30. VALENTÍA   _____

Puzzle 5: Scramble Fill-In

To solve this fill-in puzzle, "translate" the 20 English words into Spanish, but not for meaning. Rearrange each English word to form a common Spanish word. After you successfully anagram them, enter them into the grid. More than one word may fit in a given location, but the overall solution is unique. Note that some of the Spanish words may contain accent marks even though their English equivalents do not.

3 Letters

RAM
SOD

4 Letters

CODE
CONE

COOP
FACE
MAIL
POLE
REST
SAME
TEAR

5 Letters

AIMED
APPLE
BROIL
CHAFE
RAVEN
TOILS

6 Letters

IRONED
MOANED

7 Letters

ACROBAT

Puzzle 6: Coming Full Circle

Starting with the word CERO, form a word chain of four-letter words in which each word in the sequence begins with the last two letters of the word that precedes it and ends with the first two letters of the word that follows it. As an added challenge, the clues to help you identify the remaining 28 words in the chain are listed alphabetically, rather than in numerical order.

1. CERO

2. _ _ _ _

3. _ _ _ _

4. _ _ _ _

5. _ _ _ _

6. _ _ _ _

7. _ _ _ _

8. _ _ _ _

9. _ _ _ _

10. _ _ _ _

11. _ _ _ _

12. _ _ _ _

13. _ _ _ _

14. _ _ _ _

15. _ _ _ _

16. _ _ _ _

17. _ _ _ _

18. _ _ _ _

19. _ _ _ _

20. _ _ _ _

21. _ _ _ _

22. _ _ _ _

23. _ _ _ _

24. _ _ _ _

25. _ _ _ _

26. _ _ _ _

27. _ _ _ _

28. _ _ _ _

29. _ _ _ _

30. CERO

AEROSOL PARA EL PEINADO

ÁREA

BARCO GRANDE

BARRO

BORRADOR

CALIFICACIÓN

CILINDRO DE CERA

CINCO MÁS UNO

CUCHILLO AGUDO PEQUEÑO

ETAPA

EXTREMIDAD DEL BRAZO HUMANO

GANCHO PARA LEVANTAR COSAS

GRAN MASA DE AGUA DULCE

HERRAMIENTA PARA CAVAR

LECHO

MANJAR MEXICANO

MARTILLO GRUESO

MATERIAL

NINGUNA COSA

NÚMERO DE MESES EN UN AÑO

PARTE LATERAL

PRENDAS PARA VESTIRSE

PROPIEDAD DE UNA NOVIA

SACERDOTE TIBETANO

SEMEJANTE AL TERCIOPELO

SINIESTRO

TIERRA RODEADA DE AGUA

VASO CON PIE

Puzzle 7: Anagram Crossword

The clues to this puzzle are anagrams of the Spanish words that you enter in this crossword grid. For example, for the clue "Enumerar o narrar," you might enter the word CONTRA, which can be formed by rearranging the letters of CONTAR. Some words may have more than one anagram (in this case, CONTAR can also form CARTÓN, CORTÁN, and TRANCO), but only one word for each clue correctly links up with all the other words.

Hint: You may need to add, move, or remove accent marks in the anagrammed word to be entered in the grid.

Across

3 FRUTA ROJA

4 BARCO PARA NOÉ Y LOS ANIMALES

6 MUJER QUE VIVE EN UN CONVENTO

7 INTERPRETA UN PAPEL EN EL TEATRO

9 TRABAJO

10 COMER LA COMIDA DE NOCHE

12 CARRETERA O VÍA

15 DIECISÉIS ONZAS

16 CAPITAL DE ITALIA

17 LOS ESTADOS UNIDOS, EN COMPARACIÓN CON MÉXICO

19 CARNE DE CERDO

20 HOMBRE DE OZ, EN LITERATURA

21 DE TOKIO O KIOTO

22 ELECTRODOMÉSTICO QUE GUARDA LA COMIDA FRÍA

Down

1 TIEMPOS ENTRE MAÑANAS Y NOCHES

2 COMIDA DE NOCHE

5 MUJER RECIÉN CASADA

6 INSTRUMENTO DE CUERDA

8 HOGAR DE REYES Y REINAS

11 NÚMERO DE ESTACIONES

13 LUGAR PARA VER PELÍCULAS

14 PARIENTE MASCULINO

18 ANIMAL EN UNA CORRIDA

19 DOMINIO DE UN DENTISTA

Puzzle 8: Compound Fractures

Most Spanish compounds take the form verb + noun, such as ROMPECABEZAS, which means "puzzle" and translates literally as "it breaks heads." In this puzzle, we've disassembled common Spanish words into two components, neither of which is semantically related to the word it forms. In the example below, by joining ALGO (something) and DON (mister), you can form the word ALGODÓN (cotton). Note that in this example, the newly formed word has an accent mark, whereas neither of its individual components do; accents may either be added or removed when forming the larger word.

~~ALGO~~	DURA	PERA	TAXIS
ARIA	EDAD	POR	TÉ
BAZA	EN	PULMÓN	TENDER
CALA	ES	RIEGO	TERCIO
CAMA	FEO	SAL	TODA
CAPO	IDA	SASTRE	VA
CARA	LOCO ·	SIN	VER
CON	MÁS	SOL	VÍA
DE	MOTOR	SOLA	
~~DON~~	PELO	SUELO	

 ALGODÓN _____ _____

_____ _____ _____

_____ _____ _____

_____ _____ _____

_____ _____ _____

_____ _____

Puzzle 9: Wordplay Categories

Below is a list of 27 Spanish words. Twenty-five of them can be arranged into five categories of five words each based on a common bond involving some form of wordplay. For example, the words ALA, ENE, ORO, ROTOR, and SERES are all palindromes — that is, they are spelled the same way forwards and backwards. The two remaining words form an apt phrase for you upon completing the puzzle.

AMA	HATO	NOS	TERSA
ARTES	INMATERIAL	NUEVO	TESAR
BOVINO	JAGUAR	OBRA	TRABAJO
BUEN	LAVA	RAYÓN	TRACE
ESCOLAR	LEER	RESTA	TREN
ESTAR	MAYOR	SOY	VIENTO
FLECHERO	MEDIA	TEN	

_____	_____	_____
_____	_____	
_____	_____	_____
_____	_____	
_____	_____	_____
_____	_____	
_____	_____	_____
_____	_____	
_____	_____	_____
_____	_____	

Puzzle 10: Cryptocrossword

This is a regular crossword puzzle — with one difference. It comes with an encoded answer grid. After you enter the answer to a clue in the blank grid, use the code in the answer grid to insert that same letter everywhere it appears in the puzzle. Every letter of the alphabet — including K and W, but not Ñ — appears in the solution at least twice.

Across

3 NINGUNA COSA

6 PALO BLANCO PARA LA PIZARRA

7 OPORTUNO

8 GRAN CANTIDAD

11. A MENUDO

14 EXPRESIÓN CORTÉS PARA HACER UNA DEMANDA

16 LAVAMANOS

17 PABELLÓN DE VENTA PEQUEÑO

19 COMPAÑERO

21 ALEGRÍA

22 BARRITA DE GRAFITO

Down

1 RESULTADO FELIZ

2 APERTURA ORAL

3 VÍNCULO

4 AL INTERIOR

5 TRASLADARSE DE UN LUGAR A OTRO

9 EXISTE

10 PLANTA DE TAMAÑO PEQUEÑO

12 CONJUNTO DEPORTIVO

13 FRUTA DE LA GALLINA

15 MÁQUINA PARA MEDIR EL TIEMPO

17 AVE NEOZELANDESA

18 ÓRGANO DE VISTA

20 PUNTO EN FÚTBOL

Solutions

Puzzle 1

1. **SER**VILLETA (napkin), ME**SER**O (waiter), CON**SER**VACIÓN (conservation)

2. CA**MAR**ERO (waiter, steward), A**MAR**ILLO (yellow), **MAR**TES (Tuesday)

3. BA**SURA** (garbage), **SUR**FISTA (surfer), ME**SUR**ADO (moderate, restrained)

4. CO**MES**TIBLE (edible), CUBRE**MES**A (tabletopper), **MES**ONCILLO (small restaurant)

5. **SAL**ARIO (salary), EN**SAL**ADA (salad), **SAL**UD (health)

6. **POR**TAL (doorway), DE**POR**TES (sports), O**POR**TUNA (timely, appropriate)

7. **SIN**GULAR (singular), CAMPE**SIN**O (peasant), **SIN**AGOGA (synagogue)

8. DOSCIEN**TOS** (two hundred), COS**TOS**O (costly), O**TOS**COPIO (otoscope)

9. CAM**PAN**A (bell), **PAN**TALLA (screen), EM**PAN**ADA (individual turnover-like pastry)

10. BOS**QUE** (forest), RI**QUE**ZA (richness, wealth), **QUE**SO (cheese)

Puzzle 2

One of the words at 6 Across, ÑAME (Spanish for yam) is one of only a few Spanish words that begin with the letter Ñ. Others include ÑU (gnu), ÑANDÚ (ostrich), and ÑOCLO (macaroon).

Puzzle 3

4 Letters: BOCA, BREA, CABO, CARO (CARA), CARA, OBRA, OLLA, ROCA

5 Letters: BARCA, BELLO (BELLA), CABER, CALLE, CEBRA, CLARO (CLARA), COBRA, COBRE, ROBLE

6 Letters: COLLAR

7 Letters: CABALLO, CABELLO, CEBOLLA

9 Letters: CABALLERO

Puzzle 4

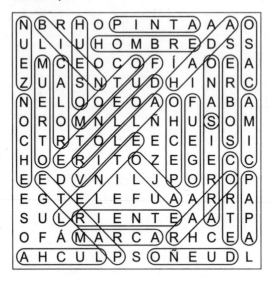

The first word listed is the answer to the numbered clue; the second one is the word located in the grid.

1. JUEGO/FUEGO
2. JUEZ/NUEZ
3. DUCHA/LUCHA
4. PUENTE/FUENTE
5. COCHE/NOCHE
6. COLOR/DOLOR
7. MENTE/LENTE
8. NOMBRE/HOMBRE
9. MANO/SANO
10. CARO/RARO
11. MARTE/PARTE
12. CINTA/PINTA
13. FOTO/MOTO
14. SUEÑO/DUEÑO
15. MAPA/PAPA

16. QUESO/HUESO
17. SILLA/VILLA
18. DIENTE/RIENTE
19. BARCA/MARCA
20. POBRE/SOBRE
21. TIERRA/SIERRA
22. CIEN/BIEN
23. NORTE/CORTE
24. NADA/HADA
25. OJO/AJO
26. PUERTO/MUERTO
27. VASO/CASO
28. RIMA/CIMA
29. TECHO/PECHO
30. VALOR/CALOR

Puzzle 5

Puzzle 6

1. CERO
2. ROPA
3. PANA
4. NAVE
5. VELA
6. LAGO
7. GOMA
8. MANO
9. NOTA
10. TACO
11. COPA
12. PALA
13. LADO
14. DOTE
15. TELA

16. LACA
17. CAMA
18. MAZO
19. ZONA
20. NADA
21. DAGA
22. GAFA
23. FASE
24. SEIS
25. ISLA
26. LAMA
27. MALO
28. LODO
29. DOCE
30. CERO

Puzzle 7

The answers to the crossword clues follow. The words in parentheses appear in the grid.

Across

3 FRESA (FRASE)
4 ARCA (CARA)
6 MONJA (JAMÓN)
7 ACTOR (TOCAR)
9 LABOR (ÁRBOL)
10 CENAR (NACER)
12 CAMINO (CAMIÓN)
15 LIBRA (ABRIL)
16 ROMA (AMOR)
17 NORTE (TERNO)
19 PUERCO (CUERPO)
20 MAGO (GOMA)
21 JAPONÉS (ESPONJA)
22 FRIGO (GRIFO)

Down

1 TARDES (DETRÁS)
2 CENA (ACNÉ)
5 NOVIA (AVIÓN)
6 BANJO (JABÓN)
8 CASTILLO (COSTILLA)
11 CUATRO (CUARTO)
13 CINE (CIEN)
14 PADRE (PARED)
18 TORO (ROTO)
19 BOCA (CABO)

Puzzle 8

Answers in alphabetical order: ALGODÓN, CALABAZA, CAMAFEO, CAPOTE, CONSUELO, DESASTRE, ENTENDER, ESPERA, LOCOMOTOR, MÁSCARA, PULMONARIA, SALIDA, SINTAXIS, SOLARIEGO, SOLEDAD, TERCIOPELO, TODAVÍA, VAPOR, VERDURA.

Puzzle 9

The 27 words can be grouped as follows:

ARTES, ESTAR, RESTA, TERSA, and TESAR are all anagrams of each other.

AMA, HATO, LAVA, OBRA, and RAYÓN can all form Spanish words by placing the letter C at the front: CAMA, CHATO, CLAVA, COBRA, and CRAYÓN.

BOVINO, ESCOLAR, FLECHERO, INMATERIAL, and JAGUAR contain the words for beverages hidden in their letters: VINO, COLA, LECHE, MATE, and AGUA.

NOS, NUEVO, TRACE, TREN, and VIENTO can have one letter changed to form the word for a number: DOS, NUEVE, TRECE, TRES, and CIENTO.

LEER, MAYOR, MEDIA, SOY, and TEN are spelled the same as English words but are not direct cognates.

The remaining two words form the phrase ¡BUEN TRABAJO!

Puzzle 10

Chapter 12

Ten Tools for Building Your Spanish Capabilities

In This Chapter

▶ Preparing yourself to soak up Spanish

▶ Getting results from your efforts

▶ Enjoying your new skills

*Y*ou remember something better when you encounter it in a fun format or context. We explain that concept in Chapter 1, and certainly we hope you enjoy the puzzles and games throughout this book — and come away from them with improved Spanish skills.

Discovering something new is always exciting and beneficial, but a little bit of discipline gives your new skills staying power over the long run. In this chapter, you find ten tried-and-true tools for keeping your Spanish skills in top-notch condition.

Practice! Practice! Practice!

You just can't overdose on practice. What you don't use, you lose, and nowhere is this more true than when dealing with a foreign language.

Like a concert pianist, you have to make time to go over your skills every day. And we mean *all* the skills: speaking, reading, and writing.

Take advantage of every opportunity to use your Spanish. For example:

  ✔ Order that *tostada* with confidence and careful pronunciation.

  ✔ When you see the turnoff for "Boca Raton" on your next Florida excursion, trill your R with pride.

✔ Write out your grocery list using Spanish words for the items
you need.

✔ Greet politely and chat up those nice ladies at the bus stop
who seem to be having a friendly *charla*.

✔ Next time you rent a DVD, turn on the Spanish subtitles and
follow along to get an entirely new take on what the actors are
saying and to see how well the captioners captured the spirit
of the dialog.

Bring Spanish into your life in some way every day.

Make Your Own Flash Cards

Flash cards are a fantastic and economical way to learn vocabulary. All you need is a package of blank 3x5 cards and a pen. Put
the Spanish word on one side and its English equivalent on the
other. You can buy preprinted flash cards, but making your own
gives you a double benefit because you reinforce your learning by
writing out the items yourself.

Set aside at least five minutes per day to study the cards. Begin by
reading the Spanish word out loud in the best pronunciation you
can, and then test yourself by saying the English equivalent; check
yourself by turning over the card to see whether you're correct.
After you go through the assigned cards, shuffle them well, and
then repeat the same procedure beginning with the English side
this time. You can use this process for identifying masculine and
feminine words, verb tense conjugations — anything you need to
reinforce. (When Leslie was a student, she highlighted the masculine words in blue, the feminine words in pink, and the irregular
verbs in orange to help her remember those aspects.)

After a while, you're going to have a rather large, unwieldy collec-
tion of cards. You can put aside those items you've mastered, but
once every three weeks or so, bring out those stored cards and
shuffle them into the current deck. If you forget a meaning or miss
a conjugation, then that retired card should go into the active pile
until your next big card review.

Read Aloud to Hear Your Own Voice

You learn to speak by speaking and to recognize different auditory
patterns by listening closely and often. If you want to hone your

speaking and listening skills, read aloud in Spanish. At the beginning, you're going to sound like the worst *gringo* used car salesman on late-night Spanish-language TV, but that's OK! You want to exercise that mouth and tongue and get used to hearing your voice saying unfamiliar sound patterns and words. In a very short period of time, we assure you, you'll be able to correct yourself and be on the road to a native pronunciation.

Say out loud the Spanish words in the puzzles and games you complete in this book. If you're using a textbook, read aloud the Spanish exercises, conversation selections, and culture nuggets that you go over in class each day. Write some simple sentences, and then say them out loud to train your ear as well as your tongue.

Write Out Class Notes Daily

By writing out the notes you take in class, not only do you give yourself an instant review of that day's lesson, but you reinforce your writing and reading skills. Rewriting your notes sharpens your brain, provides continuity to your lesson, clarifies important concepts, and gives you a clear reference from which to study for exams and complete homework assignments. When that final exam comes around, you have a leg up on everyone else because you won't have to cram at the last minute — you've been reviewing every day and seeing the lesson in your own words, not to mention honing that visual part of your brain to give yourself a picture of that information in your mind's eye.

Seek Out a Practice Buddy

When it comes to language study, two (or three or four) heads are better than one! Making the time commitment to practice with another person does wonders for your language skills. You get the chance to speak, rehearse new elements, and listen to someone else's pronunciation, further enhancing your auditory skills. You can correct each other's mistakes. You can discuss and analyze class concepts and teach each other. After a while, you can actually converse in simple Spanish about current events of the day — local, national, or international — and put some real analytical thought to it.

If you're lucky enough to have access to a native Spanish speaker who's willing to practice with you, you have a treasure more precious than diamonds. Working on your skills with a native speaker is almost as good as traveling to a Spanish-speaking country. (And it's much cheaper!) Consider it immersion without the emaciation of your bank account!

This Is a Stick-Up! Use Sticky Notes

Sticky notes are flash cards that are constantly on display. Use them to reinforce vocabulary for things around you. Put the words *el espejo* on a sticky note and then put it on the bathroom mirror. Every morning when you brush your teeth, you see that little note and make the connection between *espejo* and mirror. (While you're at it, put on one with *el cepillo de dientes* on the toothbrush holder.)

When you encounter one of your sticky notes, say the words out loud! Do so, and you get visual, phonetic, and auditory reinforcement from one little piece of paper.

Use sticky notes anywhere you spend time. Try them at work — *teléfono, teclado, engrampador.* (You get extra reinforcement from writing the words out yourself.) In the kitchen, look at the posted words *estufa, gabinete,* and *horno de microondas* while you prepare the salad. Surround yourself with Spanish!

Be a Spanish Language Media Hound

Spanish media is a multibillion-dollar business. Almost 450 million people around the world speak Spanish, and so you can easily find media tailored to reach all those people. If you live in a large metropolitan area, chances are excellent that local Spanish-language TV and radio stations, as well as Spanish-language newspapers and magazines, are available to you. The major satellite and cable TV systems worldwide carry Spanish-language programming, as well.

Take every opportunity to access whatever Spanish-language offerings you find. Watch the commercials in Spanish for nationally branded things like detergents, diapers, cooking oil, and beer — many of them are word-for-word translations of the English commercials you know and love (well, maybe not love but tolerate).

Commercials are a great place to start listening to Spanish because the words for the products are repeated over and over and so are easy to catch. Adam found that watching two newscasts a night — one in English followed by one in Spanish — helped him absorb a lot of vocabulary simply by hearing the Spanish words and by connecting them to the information he'd already heard in English.

Look for Spanish from these and other sources:

- ✔ Watch a *telenovela* and be amazed by how much you understand.

- ✔ Pick up a Spanish-language newspaper and read the headlines, comics, and classified ads.

- ✔ Listen to the happy dance tunes and soulful ballads on Spanish radio, keeping an ear open for words you recognize in the lyrics.

- ✔ Buy a CD of popular Spanish music from Latino singers like Julio and Enrique Iglesias, Linda Ronstadt, Shakira, Gloria Estefan, Juan Gabriel, or Christina Aguilera. Music is an excellent and enjoyable way to learn another language! (Often, the liner notes of the CD contain the Spanish lyrics so you can follow along; in a few lucky cases, you also get an English translation.)

- ✔ Rent a DVD and watch a Spanish-language movie.

- ✔ Pick up a popular Hollywood release and set the subtitles or spoken language on Spanish. Cartoons, children's movies, and feature animation are especially good for improving your Spanish.

You can improve your Spanish just by paying attention. Music, movies, newspapers, and other media give you a great opportunity to absorb the language in interesting ways with immediate results.

Focus on Your Interests and Goals

If you're really determined to master Spanish, you need to focus on what you want to know and how you want to use it. Maybe you want to

- ✔ Travel

- ✔ Conduct business

- ✔ Communicate with the community

- ✔ Fulfill a graduation requirement

- ✔ Teach Spanish to others

- ✔ Be ready for a medical or emergency situation

- ✔ Get in touch with your heritage

- ✔ Study abroad

- ✔ Retire and live the good life on a beach in Mallorca

- ✔ Read *Cien Años de Soledad* in the original Spanish

Each of the above scenarios requires a different type of knowledge and study. Zero in on what you want to get out of Spanish and focus on those things that will help you achieve that goal. Don't spend inordinate amounts of time learning grammatical vocabulary, for example, if you want to work at a doctor's office.

Emphasize the vocabulary, phrases, and structures that best suit your needs. Don't get sidetracked with themes or terminology that take up your time and brain space without enhancing your desired outcome.

Don't Worry about Making Mistakes!

No doubt you mispronounced and misformed many words on the road to English proficiency, but you didn't let that stop you from talking a blue streak. Sure, parents and teachers corrected you along the way, you filed their tips away for future reference, and you listened to grown-ups speaking properly. You figured out how to communicate in English without being embarrassed.

You can't make an omelet unless you break some eggs, and you can't grasp Spanish properly and well without making some mistakes. Everybody makes them, even the class valedictorian.

Chances are good that someone will correct you when you make a mistake. If you speak without being corrected or receiving a quizzical look, then you have made yourself understood. Congratulations!

When you recognize your mistakes and make efforts to correct them, either immediately or in the future, you've reached a huge developmental milestone. Pat yourself on the back!

Experience has shown us that using our Spanish opens so many doors and helps make friendly connections, regardless of the grammatical errors we make. We also find that Spanish speakers are extremely proud of their linguistic and cultural heritage, and they're thrilled when someone outside of that culture takes the time and effort to learn about it. The smiles they show are heartwarming and memorable, and they'll bend over backward to help you to understand and be understood.

If you make your best effort to connect with native Spanish speakers, regardless of your abilities, your rewards will be of value beyond words.

Take Your Act on the Road!

We saved this tip for last because it's the most rewarding and enriching. Travel to a Spanish-speaking country, and you are immersed in the language and the culture, just as if you had been born there. No other language-learning method equals full immersion. You hear the beautiful accents and intonations, catchphrases, everyday banter, and laughter that simply can't be taught in a classroom or a book.

You may have the fundamentals of the verbs and vocabulary to get around and function reasonably well, but being among the natives adds a spice, richness, and finesse to your language. Your ear-training, pronunciation, and fluency grow exponentially in a very short time. You see the world through different eyes. As the German philosopher and poet Goethe said, "To acquire a second language is to acquire a second self."

siness/Accounting Bookkeeping
okkeeping For Dummies
8-0-7645-9848-7

ay Business
-in-One For Dummies,
d Edition
8-0-470-38536-4

b Interviews
r Dummies,
Edition
8-0-470-17748-8

sumes For Dummies,
Edition
8-0-470-08037-5

ck Investing
r Dummies,
Edition
8-0-470-40114-9

ccessful Time
nagement
r Dummies
8-0-470-29034-7

mputer Hardware
ckBerry For Dummies,
Edition
8-0-470-45762-7

mputers For Seniors
r Dummies
8-0-470-24055-7

one For Dummies,
d Edition
8-0-470-42342-4

Laptops For Dummies,
3rd Edition
978-0-470-27759-1

Macs For Dummies,
10th Edition
978-0-470-27817-8

Cooking & Entertaining
Cooking Basics
For Dummies,
3rd Edition
978-0-7645-7206-7

Wine For Dummies,
4th Edition
978-0-470-04579-4

Diet & Nutrition
Dieting For Dummies,
2nd Edition
978-0-7645-4149-0

Nutrition For Dummies,
4th Edition
978-0-471-79868-2

Weight Training
For Dummies,
3rd Edition
978-0-471-76845-6

Digital Photography
Digital Photography
For Dummies,
6th Edition
978-0-470-25074-7

Photoshop Elements 7
For Dummies
978-0-470-39700-8

Gardening
Gardening Basics
For Dummies
978-0-470-03749-2

Organic Gardening
For Dummies,
2nd Edition
978-0-470-43067-5

Green/Sustainable
Green Building
& Remodeling
For Dummies
978-0-4710-17559-0

Green Cleaning
For Dummies
978-0-470-39106-8

Green IT For Dummies
978-0-470-38688-0

Health
Diabetes For Dummies,
3rd Edition
978-0-470-27086-8

Food Allergies
For Dummies
978-0-470-09584-3

Living Gluten-Free
For Dummies
978-0-471-77383-2

Hobbies/General
Chess For Dummies,
2nd Edition
978-0-7645-8404-6

Drawing For Dummies
978-0-7645-5476-6

Knitting For Dummies,
2nd Edition
978-0-470-28747-7

Organizing For Dummies
978-0-7645-5300-4

SuDoku For Dummies
978-0-470-01892-7

Home Improvement
Energy Efficient Homes
For Dummies
978-0-470-37602-7

Home Theater
For Dummies,
3rd Edition
978-0-470-41189-6

Living the Country
Lifestyle
All-in-One For Dummies
978-0-470-43061-3

Solar Power Your Home
For Dummies
978-0-470-17569-9

ailable wherever books are sold. For more information or to order direct: U.S. customers visit www.dummies.com or call 1-877-762-2974.
. customers visit www.wileyeurope.com or call (0) 1243 843291. Canadian customers visit www.wiley.ca or call 1-800-567-4797.

Internet

Blogging For Dummies,
2nd Edition
978-0-470-23017-6

eBay For Dummies,
6th Edition
978-0-470-49741-8

Facebook For Dummies
978-0-470-26273-3

Google Blogger
For Dummies
978-0-470-40742-4

Web Marketing
For Dummies,
2nd Edition
978-0-470-37181-7

WordPress For Dummies,
2nd Edition
978-0-470-40296-2

Language & Foreign Language

French For Dummies
978-0-7645-5193-2

Italian Phrases
For Dummies
978-0-7645-7203-6

Spanish For Dummies
978-0-7645-5194-9

Spanish For Dummies,
Audio Set
978-0-470-09585-0

Macintosh

Mac OS X Snow Leopard
For Dummies
978-0-470-43543-4

Math & Science

Algebra I For Dummies
978-0-7645-5325-7

Biology For Dummies
978-0-7645-5326-4

Calculus For Dummies
978-0-7645-2498-1

Chemistry For Dummies
978-0-7645-5430-8

Microsoft Office

Excel 2007 For Dummies
978-0-470-03737-9

Office 2007 All-in-One
Desk Reference
For Dummies
978-0-471-78279-7

Music

Guitar For Dummies,
2nd Edition
978-0-7645-9904-0

iPod & iTunes
For Dummies,
6th Edition
978-0-470-39062-7

Piano Exercises
For Dummies
978-0-470-38765-8

Parenting & Education

Parenting For Dummies,
2nd Edition
978-0-7645-5418-6

Type 1 Diabetes
For Dummies
978-0-470-17811-9

Pets

Cats For Dummies,
2nd Edition
978-0-7645-5275-5

Dog Training For Dummies,
2nd Edition
978-0-7645-8418-3

Puppies For Dummies,
2nd Edition
978-0-470-03717-1

Religion & Inspiration

The Bible For Dummies
978-0-7645-5296-0

Catholicism For Dummies
978-0-7645-5391-2

Women in the Bible
For Dummies
978-0-7645-8475-6

Self-Help & Relationship

Anger Management
For Dummies
978-0-470-03715-7

Overcoming Anxiety
For Dummies
978-0-7645-5447-6

Sports

Baseball For Dummies,
3rd Edition
978-0-7645-7537-2

Basketball For Dummies
2nd Edition
978-0-7645-5248-9

Golf For Dummies,
3rd Edition
978-0-471-76871-5

Web Development

Web Design All-in-One
For Dummies
978-0-470-41796-6

Windows Vista

Windows Vista
For Dummies
978-0-471-75421-3

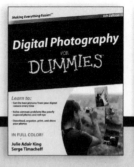

Available wherever books are sold. For more information or to order direct: U.S. customers visit www.dummies.com or call 1-877-762-29
U.K. customers visit www.wileyeurope.com or call (0) 1243 843291. Canadian customers visit www.wiley.ca or call 1-800-567-4797.